Laity today

A series of Studies edited by
the Pontifical Council for the Laity

PONTIFICIUM CONSILIUM PRO LAICIS

THE WORLD OF SPORT TODAY
A FIELD OF CHRISTIAN MISSION

International Seminar

Vatican, 11-12 November 2005

LIBRERIA EDITRICE VATICANA
2006

Cover photo: *Courtesy of the Italian Sports Centre*

ISBN 88-209-7863-6

www.libreriaeditricevaticana.com

PREFACE

The practice of sport, which dates back to the dawn of human history, has now become firmly established as a mass phenomenon without equal precedent. According to some scholars, sport's capacity to engage huge crowds of people on a planetary scale, and to straddle geographic, social, economic and language barriers, makes it one of the most universally recognised components of popular culture.[1]

The emotional – and not infrequently "all-embracing" – involvement that practising sport and watching sports events can generate, coupled with the process of globalisation and modern communications technologies, makes this a force that produces powerful experiences, but also gives rise to serious risks. Today, sport is in the hands of an influential and lucrative "leisure industry" which produces dreams of power and success in millions of individuals. Sport is often experienced as a kind of "ecstasy", a way of evading the drabness of daily life. It has been said that in sport we can recover a euphoric sense of wholeness, autonomy and power that are often denied in the humdrum routine which is the destiny of most men and women.[2] In many people's lives, sport has acquired an importance that goes beyond that of mere amusement or entertainment. For many of our contemporaries sport has become a way of life, an essential element for meeting basic needs,

[1] Cf. T. MILLER-G. LAWRENCE-J. McKAY, D. ROWE, *Globalization and Sport: Playing the World*, London 2001.
[2] A. GUTTMAN, *From Ritual to Record*, New York 1978, 157.

such as self-esteem and self-fulfilment, and a factor that not only determines a sense of identity and belonging, but also the meaning of life itself. And that is not all: sport has become, in every respect, a surrogate for religious experience.[3] It is a paradoxical fact that, in our secularised society, sports events have taken on the character of collective rituals, fraught with emotion. Stadiums and gymnasiums are like temples to this "new religion". And this process, which is typical of our present age, is accompanied by radical changes in relations between people and their bodies. For we have moved beyond concern for personal health and personal grooming to the worship of the body and its physical dimension.[4] In order to build up an image that is compliant with the canons of prevailing contemporary thinking, no sacrifice is too much to pay, and people do not hesitate to undergo strenuous physical exercise, rigorous diets, and even hazardous pharmacological and surgical treatments. The body has now become a raw material to be fashioned at will, following the absolute dictates of the current fad.

Our post-modern culture has become embroiled in a crisis that empties it of value only to fill it with the non-values that come from a nihilistic mentality that reduces the meaning of human life to an unbridled search for pleasure and consumption. This has far-reaching repercussions on the world of sport. Far from being used to achieve the healthy growth of the individual person, the practice of sport is increasingly threatening people; rather than directing them towards freedom, it is increasingly enslaving them, to themselves, to imposed fads and fashions, and to the interests which are concealed behind sports events.[5] The causes of this process, which are robbing sport of

---

[3] Cf. T. MILLER-G. LAWRENCE-J. MCKAY, D. ROWE, *Globalization and Sport: Playing the World*, London 2001.

[4] PIUS XII made a robust response to this tendency when he said "care for the body, strengthening of the body -yes; but cult of the body, making a god of the body -no". (cf. R. FEENEY, *A Catholic Perspective: Physical Exercise and Sports*, Aquinas Press, Virginia 1995, 48).

[5] Cf. P. JAKOBI-H.E. RÖSCH, *Sport und Menschnwürde*, Mainz 1982.

its true nature, are manifold.[6] One of the most important and prominent causes is the way the world of sport is being conditioned by the new overarching laws of the market. The economic dimension, which has been present in sport from the earliest times, is now predominant, with the result that sport is seen today as a branch of the economy in its own right.[7] Sport has become a big business, with all the negative consequences this entails. The spectacularization of sport has made it one more consumption commodity among so many others – in this instance, the consumption of results and records. This explains the quest for victory at all cost, even if by unlawful means. Doping and anabolic steroids are no longer newsworthy because they are so widely used. Yet they threaten the very sense of competitive sport while attacking the dignity of the human person, who is considered as a mere instrument, solely used to guarantee the maximum performance possible, regardless of human limits. Then there are ideological and political forms of interference, when performance in a sport is considered to be a sign of the superiority of a particular political system or country. This is where, instead of uniting, sports competitions become a factor of division and conflict, not only between competing teams but also between nations. Not to mention the very serious threat looming over the sporting world of competitiveness pushed to extremes, not infrequently leading to serious acts of violence.

However, today's sport must not be viewed merely in terms of abuse and deviance. We must resist the temptation to condemn it across the board. After all, the depressing picture of the evils that afflict this vast and diverse universe are only part of the story. For the world of sport still has its sound environments and still has generous people who striving to reclaim the ideal of sport as a real school of humanity, virtue and life. These are important signs of hope, and not only for the future of sport. They must therefore not be neglected. For in sport, too, what is

---

[6] Cf. K. BAUMGARTNER – F. ENZ, "Glaube und Selbstverwirklichung im Sport", in: P. JAKOBI-H.-E. RÖSCH, *Sport und Religion*, 77-102.

[7] Cf. M. AIELLO, *Viaggio nello sport attraverso i secoli*, Le Monnier, Firenze 2004, 285-290.

above all at stake are humanity and culture, and culture is the indispensable substrate that underpins a truly human life.

In the lively debate on sport – in which sociologists, psychologists, anthropologists, and radio, television and newspaper journalists are involved, in addition to ordinary sports fans – the Church has certainly spoken out with authority. Of all the Pontiffs of the 20th century who have addressed the world of sport, John Paul II stands out for the great attention he paid to sport and to the body.[8] Not only did he speak about sport, he even practised it after becoming pope. This is why in his meetings with sports men and women, his speeches on the subject have always had a special value. Athletes saw him to be a man who truly shared their experience.

John Paul II addressed the problem of sport with great realism. He was well aware that "In addition to a sport that helps people, there is another that harms them; in addition to a sport that enhances the body, there is another that degrades it and betrays it; in addition to a sport that pursues noble ideals, there is another that looks only for profit; in addition to a sport that unites, there is another that divides".[9] He was deeply convinced that, despite this ambivalence, practising sport must be considered not only as a source of physical well-being but also as an ideal of a courageous, positive, optimistic life, and as a means whereby individuals and society can fully renew themselves.[10] John Paul II always forcefully emphasised the educational value of sport, which can inculcate such important values as love of life, spirit of sacrifice, fair play, perseverance, respect for others, friendship, sharing and solidarity.[11]

---

[8] Cf. W. Schwank, "Die Entwicklung des Sportverständnisses in päpstlichen Verlautbarungen", in: P. Jakobi-H.-E. Rösch, *Sport und Religion*, loc. cit. pp. 254-280.

[9] John Paul II, *Address to the International Convention on Sport: Sport can help build civil society*, "L'Osservatore Romano" Weekly English Edition, n. 46, November 15, 2000, 9.

[10] John Paul II, *Address to members of the Italian Sports Centre: Called to be Christ's witnesses in Sport*, "L'Osservatore Romano" Weekly English Edition, n. 28, July 14, 2004, 3.

[11] John Paul II, *Homily at the Jubilee for the Word of Sport: Even the greatest champions need Christ*, "L'Osservatore Romano" Weekly English Edition, n. 44, November 1, 2000, 1.

To achieve these lofty objectives sport nevertheless needs to discover its deepest ethos, and comply with the basic principle of the primacy of the human person. He therefore urged people to adopt a healthy approach to sport, so that sport is not practised as an end in itself, giving rise to the danger of becoming a vain and harmful idol,[12] but to make it a meaningful instrument for the comprehensive development of the person and the construction of a society made more to the measure of man. "When understood in this way, sport is not an end, but a means; it can become a vehicle of civility and genuine recreation, encouraging people to put the best of themselves on the field and to avoid what might be dangerous or seriously harmful to themselves or to others".[13] In other words, for John Paul II, the world of sport is an important areopagus of modern times, awaiting apostles who are ready to boldly announce the gospel of Jesus Christ.

And it was precisely the relationship between sport and evangelisation that was chosen as the theme of the International Seminar on "The world of sport today: a field of Christian mission", the proceedings of which are published in this volume. The seminar was held in Rome November 11-12, 2005 under the auspices of the Pontifical Council for the Laity, and officially inaugurated the work of the "Church and sport" Section of the Pontifical Council that was begun in 2004 at the request of John Paul II. It was established as a point of reference within the Holy See for all national and international sports organisations, and to act as a kind of "observatory" for the world of sport at the service of evangelisation, which is the Church's fundamental task.

The first part of the seminar which took a historical view of sport from ancient times until today, was given by Maria Aiello, an expert in

---

[12] Cf. JOHN PAUL II, *Address to conference of sports and ethics: sports can be viewed as a service to mankind.* "L'Osservatore Romano" Weekly English Edition, n. 2, January 8, 1990, 5.

[13] JOHN PAUL II, *Address to the International Convention on Sport: Sport can help build civil society,* "L'Osservatore Romano" Weekly English Edition, n. 46, November 15, 2000, 9.

9

the history of sport and sports law. She addressed a number of issues regarding the origins of sport: the linkage between physical exercise and education, the framing of sports law, relations with politics, the ever-increasing importance of the political implications of sport, and essential ethical demands. She was followed by Professor Dietmar Mieth, Professor of Moral Theology at Tübingen University (Germany), who spoke about sport in contemporary society and culture, emphasising the values and principles that are essential for framing a Christian ethos of sport. These two addresses were followed by a round table on the "Problems and challenges of sport today" with interventions on "Sport and business", "Sport and violence", "Sport and doping", and "Sport and the media".

The second phase revolved around the opportunities which sport offers the Church to realise her evangelising mission, above all among young people. This was introduced with a talk that was entitled "Opportunities and resources for renewal in sport", given by Edio Costantini, President of the Italian Sports Centre, who addressed the educational and formative dimension of sport, also with reference to Italy's long-standing tradition of parish clubs, known as "oratories", which he holds as a viable model that can always be adapted. He was followed by Mgr. Carlo Mazza, the Director of the National Office for the Pastoral Care of Leisure Time, Tourism and Sport, within the Italian Bishops' Conference, who spoke on "Sport as viewed from the Church's Magisterium". He set out an organic summary of the popes' teaching on sport, and offered a number of stimulating guidelines for identifying new ways in which Christians can be present in this field, and for making the most of the rich patrimony of teachings and resources that already exist. Speakers at the round table on the theme "Sport: the frontier of the new evangelisation" touched on such themes as Catholic sports associations and sport chaplains, pastoral care at major sports events, and the Christian presence in sports institutions. In the debate that followed, emphasis was placed above all on the role of trainers in the human and spiritual formation of athletes, pointing out, for example, that in some countries children may only spend 20 hours a year with a catechist but more than 200 hours with a coach in the practice of sport that is managed by the local parish or a Catholic school.

As the Secretary of the Pontifical Council, Bishop Josef Clemens, pointed out in his conclusions, there is no doubt that the first step towards a more organic pastoral ministry by the Church in the world of sport must be to undertake the commitment to disseminate the principles of a sound anthropology which recognises and valorises all the dimensions of the human person.

The Seminar was attended by 45 people from 18 different countries, with different experiences in the world of sport: scholars, leaders of Catholic sports associations, professional athletes, coaches, and representatives from the Bishops' Conferences of Austria, Germany, Hungary, Italy and Poland, which have instituted "Offices for the pastoral care of sport".

The establishment of the "Church and sport" Section has been warmly welcomed by people involved in sport throughout the world who see this as a palpable sign of the Church's concern for this important dimension of contemporary culture and in recognition of sports educative potential in the development of the human person. In fact, many have written to express their desire for the Church to make a contribution to help resolve the serious problems affecting sport today. Taking account of these expectations, the Seminar also dealt with sport as a "field of mission" for Christians and for all men and women of goodwill, seeking to encourage the search for pathways that can truly restore the true face of sport, and lead it back to the lofty ideals in which sport has its roots and which have animated it throughout history.

In his Message to the 20th Winter Olympics, Benedict XVI prayed that the incarnate Word, the light of the world, "may enlighten every dimension of humanity, including sport. There is nothing human, save sin, which the Son of God by becoming flesh, has not valorised ... Sport is one of the human activities which is also waiting to be enlightened by God through Christ, so that the values it expresses may be purified and elevated at both the individual and the collective levels".[14] The Church – "expert in humanity" (Paul VI) and "the Good Samaritan of humanity" (John Paul II) – is called to bring the light of Christ above all to those places where humanity runs the risk of getting lost, compromising the talents with which the Creator has endowed it.

✝ Staniśoo Ryłko

President
of the Pontifical Council for the Laity

---

[14] BENEDICT XVI, *Message for the 20th Winter Olympic Games in Turin, Italy: A light for sports,* "L'Osservatore Romano" Weekly English Edition, n. 6, February 8, 2006, 2.

12

A brief history of sport

Maria Aiello*

The world of sport, and society in general, feel the need today for a historical and humanistic approach to sport, because the practice of sport runs the risk of being excessively constrained by the strong emphasis placed on technique (from training methods to competition strategies, materials, and even drug use/abuse) and economic considerations, that is to say, viewing sport as a business. Sport cannot survive for long purely on technique and money. Today we can see shortcomings and contradictions emerging in the world of sport which demand a value-based approach which, in turn, also requires a reference to the history of sport.

A historical overview can therefore be a valid contribution to a sports culture: indeed, in ancient Greece, sport came into being and developed in close connection with culture. Throughout history, sport was not only conditioned by the culture of the day but was also capable of creating values that percolated through to society through sport – values such as equality, fraternity and fair play. Ancient Greece and the Middle Ages also proposed these values, at least in part. Sport is, and by its very nature always has been, about compliance with rules; but beyond that, in ancient times the prevailing idea was that sport made it possible to recover the experience of being a human community (one only has to think of the "Greek community" concept that emerged from the Olympic Games, which were panhellenic games,

* Maria Aiello graduated in Law from the Catholic University of Milan, as a specialist in Sports Law, and has lectured in the History of Sport and Sports Law at the European School of Economics. She is the author of "Viaggio nello Sport attraverso i secoli" (Le Monnier, 2004). A sports enthusiast since childhood, she has held offices in various capacities in the Italian Disabled Sport Federation.

that is to say, open to all Greeks). However, one can also see the limitations of the Greek concept, for sport was reserved for Greek men, aristocrats, and physically perfect Greeks.

At the end of the 19th century the values promoted by sport in the Classical age were once again advocated in the Olympic Charter, without the prejudices of the past. For the Charter recognised the ecumenical character of sport, affirming that all individuals had the right to practise it. In those days, as today, the values of equality, fraternity and fair play were not yet fully accepted by society, and by proposing them the Olympic movement encouraged their dissemination in a world where sport was also under pressure from a widespread élitist, if not openly racist, mentality. De Coubertin himself was not immune to such prejudices: his aversion to women competing is well-known, due to his conviction that because of women's different physiological constitution and the role they play in society, women were unsuitable to practise sport.

In the light of these reflections, we now have to recover the educational value of sport, viewed not only in terms of winning a contest or breaking records, but above all appreciated on account of its formative and educational value. In the Greek *Poleis*, sport – we are using the word "sport" for convenience here, even though we should really talk about "competing" – attributed a major role to the so-called gymnastic *paideia*, that is to say, the activity that all young people, or at least all the young aristocrats, were supposed to engage in, not only to achieve excellent competitive results, but above all to acquire a full and complete human education. Although one important aspect of the gymnastics *paideia* was its use for providing military training, its general purpose was also to educate the citizens by emphasising a close link between physical harmony and virtue (*arete*) according to the concept of *kalokagathia*, that is to say, the perfect balance between physical and spiritual beauty.

Plato emphasised the educational character of physical exercise but, as Aristotle was to do later on, he criticised excessive competition in the name of the concept of "measure", a concept that was to be taken up subsequently by Aristotle as the "golden mean". There is no doubt that the primary role of educating the human person was played by philosophy, yet both these philosophers made sport the basis not only of warrior training, but also of education for Greek citizens, and in more general terms of education for the men, because in ancient Greece the man-citizen link was inseparable.

The end of the Greek *polis* experience did not end the relationship between education and sport. In Hellenism, the place where young people practised sport – that is to say, the gymnasium – was to become a place for intellectual education more generally: athletic tracks and libraries came to occupy the same places with equal dignity, following a model that was subsequently to re-emerge in the British university campus tradition.

In Rome, too, alongside such cruel events as circus games, there were youth associations which proposed the practice of sport as an educational tool. Unfortunately, the Augustan model of the *collegia invenum* (youth associations) was to decline sharply at the end of the imperial age.

Before proceeding with this historical overview, I should like to clarify one point: historic literature usually says that at the end of antiquity, sport disappeared completely, as did *a fortiori* the link between education and the practice of sport. This is why the rebirth of the Olympic spirit at the end of the 19th century was viewed by many as a revival of the practice of ancient ideals after centuries of darkness. I believe that this interpretation falls far short of the mark, even though it is very widespread. Sport has never been ceased to be prac-tised throughout history, and there is evidence across the centuries to prove this. Some features of sport have always been present. I am thinking here of the spirit of competition, of overcoming obstacles, of achieving a result, and of the spirit of game-playing and physical effort. All of these confirm a certain historical continuity. There is no doubt that by the end of the Classical age many sports practices had sharply declined, leading to the ending of the Olympic Games at the end of the fourth century; but it is equally true to say, also at the cultural level, that the ancient world's appreciation of sport was replaced by an attitude that was even hostile to sport, not only because of the corruption of sport in late antiquity – corruption that took the form of excessive brutality and the turning of sports events into spectacular public entertainments – but also as a result of the gradual affirmation of ideas that set greater store by the spiritual dimension to the detriment of anything that had to do with the physical, material, dimension. However, the sports culture never stopped handing down his legacy. It is significant that martyrs were likened to athletes, and that chivalry, which became established in the eighth century, was known from the beginning specifically for championing such values as fairness, protecting the weak, and defending the faith. And it was precisely in the world of chivalry that young aristocrats found the source of their education, particularly youngest sons, who underwent spiritual and physical education from the age of seven which very closely resembled Aristotle's idea of the *gymnasium*, except that their education also included military training.

The Church would later criticise the mediaeval experience of tournaments on account of their gory aspects, yet the idea that sport could be a useful means, under certain conditions, of achieving the overall education of the human person remained firm. In the later Middle Ages important experiences in this direction were to emerge. One was Vittorino da Feltre's famous "Ca' Zoiosa" – "Joyous House" – in which, along the lines of ancient gymnasium, young aristocrats could grow harmoniously, combining open air physical exercise (running, jumping, swimming and other games) with study; there was also the *Contubernium*, at Ferrara, as a place for life in common, where young people wishing to embark on a public career were trained through study and the practice of sports. The conviction that a close linkage existed between sport and education was therefore constantly present, and was to become increasingly more popular, particularly after the 16th century. This was to be found in Montaigne's "Essays", in which the author proposed an educational method based on the view of the individual as a unity of body and soul, which involved physical, intellectual and moral education, equally; and then there was Locke's *"Some Thoughts Concerning Education"*, published in 1693 in which the practice of sport acquired paramount importance in the education of a gentleman.

Later on, in 18th century England, it was on the basis of these experiences that school and sport were so closely combined. The public school, which despite its name refers to a private educational establishment to educate the ruling classes, were based on very rigid programmes: the pupils were required to practise sport intensively, and to play popular games which in those days had no rules and often resulted in personal injuries, making it necessary to gradually regulate them. In the 19th century this was to lead to rule-setting for most contemporary sports. Throughout Europe, and particularly in the United Kingdom, a sports culture with original features of its own developed, leading to a new definition of sport altogether.

In the 19th century the first sports federations were established. Many technical innovations were introduced, such as goal posts for soccer, and the use of chronometers; popular sports newspapers emerged, and the first practical manuals for the training of athletes were published. In other words, sport as we know it today emerged, for which one essential condition was that only amateurs could take part, according to a fundamental principle that was a novelty at that time: the autonomy of sport. Thomas Arnold was a convinced advocate of this principle, as the headmaster of Rugby College, where sport was seen as a means of inculcating the principle of *fair play*, a competitive spirit, and at the same time a spirit of cooperation, into young men. His experience, and more generally the experience of the British model, was to influence Baron de Coubertin when he founded the modern Olympic movement.

But in the 20th century, these experiences of a strong interpenetration between sport, values and education have also been countered by trends in the opposite direction, as a result of having made sport subservient to ideas and objectives that not only have nothing to do with genuine human formation or education, but are also disquieting. For in the mid-20th century many political regimes would use sport as a means of controlling the masses and as a tool for playing power politics. The 1936 Berlin Games were a striking example of this. The Olympic movement, as I just said, was based on the idea that sport has to be totally autonomous of politics, and this independence was made all the more evident by the sharp distinction drawn between sports law and ordinary law: for the ordinary courts of law are used to deal only with general cases regarding sport, but not exclusively sports issues terms (for example, safeguarding athletes' health), whereas on purely technical matters (for example, the rules governing competitions) sports law alone is always invoked.

Fascism, Nazism and, later on, Socialism, subsequently advocated a dangerous subordination of sport and politics. Not only did sport prove incapable of controlling events – as had been the case in ancient Greece with the Olympic Truce, the so-called *ekekeiria*, under which all hostilities ceased during the Games – but it was the Olympic Games which were conditioned by hostilities.

Today, however, the problem of political control is less important. What is becoming increasingly important is economic conditioning. The link between sport, the economy and professionalism dates back to ancient times; one only has to think of sponsorship in Greece, where wealthy people invested vast sums of money for evident publicity-seeking or political purposes. So even then economic conditioning and sport were not considered incompatible; professionalism was not only accepted, but was recognised, and became standard practice. Furthermore, there was no shortage of professionals from humble backgrounds who were outstanding in classical competitive sport: Milo of Croton and Glaucus of Caristus were both professional sportsmen in the modern sense of the term. Today, sport is increasingly coming to resemble a business, with the risk of distorting the very principles of sport. One only has to recall that the 1996 Atlanta Games were the brainchild of Coca-Cola, or that the advertising industry wants soccer matches to be broken down into four 'halves' to make it easier to schedule commercial breaks.

Moreover, the increasing power of economic and financial interests, which is driving competition to its extreme limits, has given rise to yet another factor: doping. Doping existed in the ancient world, of course, and many athletes would eat certain foods, such as a specific type of mushroom, to improve their performance. But it was only in the 20th century that this was to become one of the most serious issues facing the world of sport, and one shocking example of this was the treatment of East German athletes only a few decades ago, which placed their lives in serious jeopardy. Today, unfortunately, no sports discipline can be considered exempt from doubts about fair play, the honesty of the winners, or even the health of the athletes and players. Even amateur sport, and sometimes disabled sport, have not succeeded in steering clear of this problem.

Contemporary sport would therefore appear to be in crisis, primarily in terms of its founding values. The risk of its degenerating, perhaps along the lines of what happened in the late ancient world with its violence, and the way sport was transformed into an extreme form of highly spectacular entertainment, is not a purely theoretical idea. Yet at various levels, from the Olympic movement to national governments one can see an awareness of the issues at stake, and the desire of many people to refound a new kind of sport, as a temple of values, as an instrument for educating young people and, in more general terms, educating the person *per se*. Tangible steps have been taken in this direction, such as the drafting in 2003 of a World Anti-Doping Code by Wada, an independent organisation financed by the IOC and its members (about 150).

The Magisterium of the Church also played a decisive role in the 20th century, and still does. The Church's interest in sport dates back to the dawn of Christianity: St Paul, in his letter to the Philippians, adopted a sporting metaphor: "I press on toward the goal for the prize", namely, the Kingdom of Heaven. The Fathers of the Church often referred to combat, fatigue and victory as images of the Christian life, and in the early Christian catacombs we find martyrs depicted as Christ's athletes. The Church's ideas about sport have varied throughout history keeping pace with changes in culture and society; but in the mid-20th century, she showed a much more systematic interest in the evolution of sport, introducing into it a fundamental principle: the ethical dimension. But if we view this attitude in historical terms, we can see that there has been a certain lack of continuity. For in the Middle Ages the Church was often hostile to competitive sport, on the grounds that it devalued the body of those who practised it; the Church even went so far as to condemn certain sports activities, such as tournaments and duelling, which were often based on a contempt for human life.

The late lamented John Paul II, a sportsman of proven ability, showed an extraordinary outreach to sport by interpreting it in a modern light. He emphasised the solidarity aspect of sport – through the Jubilee of Sports People, the Year of the Disabled etc – pointing out that the dignity of the body was a value that was inseparable from the practice of sport, and that the goal should be to create a new civilisation of love and fellowship. These principles should certainly be translated into concrete initiatives capable of halting the decadence of the whole system, but they inevitably give rise to contradictions and doubts. We still vividly recall the debate on whether sports events should be held on Sunday, the Christian Feast Day. What is needed today is to frame the declarations of principle laid down by the Magisterium and enshrined in the Olympic Charter – fair play, equality, union of peoples, brotherhood etc – into rules, and it is here that sport directly reaches out to law. But it is then necessary to move on from law to action, to do away with the contradictions that exist between the economy and values, between competition and fair play, and between professionalism and safeguarding human health. I am therefore referring not only to sport as it is played in parish youth clubs, which are certainly have a great historical importance and are a powerful means of educating young people, but in more general terms to the need for the sporting world to recover the values that traditionally belonged to sport, and which are at the same time consistent with Christian doctrine. In this connection I look forward to the possibility of evangelising sport and evangelising through sport. It would be interesting in this connection to examine the way the potential of the mass media might be best used to achieve this.

What I have tried to do here is show the usefulness of a historical approach to today's problems: the past is a guide to the present. But the development of this debate and any action taken as a result of it cannot ignore relations with sports organisations such as the IOC, the International Federations, the sports promotion entities and sports associations in general, or relations with national governments. And I believe we must ensure that we do not neglect relations with other cultures. For while sport is being globalised, turning it into a hub around which people meet irrespective of their differences of ethnicity, culture, religion and language, the universal character of sport also makes dialogue in diversity possible. I would like to recall the dialogue in the Middle Ages between the peoples living around the shores of the Mediterranean who, despite their religious differences and their traditions, nevertheless shared the same approach to sport and had the same view of the relationship between man and sport. This dialogue was expressed in the form of chivalry, and to a great extent through falconry, which came into being in the Islamic world and very soon spread throughout the Christian West. Against this background, a debate on sport and working out appropriate responses to contemporary issues could provide an opportunity to develop the kind of ecumenical dialogue which was so central to the pontificate of John Paul II, and which continues to remain central under the present pope.

Towards an ethic of sport in contemporary culture

DIETMAR MIETH*

L ooking back over the last 100 years, the face of sport has changed beyond recognition. Although modern sport has religious and moral roots in the original Olympic ideal of the Greeks and the Olympic movement of Coubertin, it owes a good deal to the national revival movements such as that of Jahn, the father of gymnastics, to certain educational systems (e.g. in Britain), and from the democratisation of leisure time, by which sport not only increased but became accessible to all. However, sport is now, at the beginning of this new millennium, dominated by commercialisation, the media and the medical profession. Active interest in sport for fun and passive interest in top-class sport have grown enormously. A whole industry has grown up around sport that fuels its own success: advertising and sponsorship increases demand and gives sport an enormous financial boost. Media domination of sport is increasing at the top-level of professional sport with astronomical sums spent on media marketing. There is a widening chasm between the increasing importance given to sports media and its sense of responsibility. Ideals such as "it is more important to take part than to win" or "there are higher values than success" seem to be increasingly obsolete in this context.

Although sport has always been associated with health and fitness, sports' growing partnership with the medical profession, above all in

* Professor Mieth was born in Berlin in 1940 and is presently professor in moral theology with the faculty of Catholic Theology at Eberhard Karls University in Tübingen. He is a also a frequent guest professor at the universities in Freiberg, Zurich, and Nutmeg. From 1994-2000, Dr. Mieth was a member of the European Union's EGE (European Group for Ethics in the Sciences and the New Technologies) as well as a consultant on various commissions of bioethics and medicine within the Federal Government of Germany. Among his numerous writings, Dr. Mieth is co-editor of a "Lexicon for Sport Ethics".

the area of pharmaceuticals, has brought some damaging results. Doping is something which seems to be inextricably bound with sport today. In terms of the user of controversial substances, doping is attractive. It is not just about enhancing performance, but also about relieving pain and injury, shortening recovery times and ensuring that short-term but intensive success wins over longer term participation. Doping is a very complex phenomenon even if the ban and the official fight against doping is so often reclaimed. Today, the question of aging is also often seen as related with a sportive life. The regeneration of brain cells even in the higher age by physical training has been demonstrated. Medical care has therefore grown in significance and scale. This has an impact on the products offered by the pharmaceutical industry and on the increasingly specific demands on medical personnel, for whom there is no specific training approved by sport associations or by the state.

In the end, sport mirrors our society. Its ambiguities can be looked at in the light of the broader ambiguities of our society. Yet, on the other hand, in terms of supply and demand, sport "supplies" us with a unique set of qualities or values which are attractive because they cannot be achieved (or so it appears) as efficiently by other means. Some of these values are: health and fitness, energy, the experience of competition, a feeling of achievement and success, discipline, social contact, educational and cultural opportunities, a model of fair play, solidarity, social advancement and integration.

I. Sport as a means of human development

Everyday experience shows that sport can favour human development. One of the possibilities of sport is taking part in a learning process. If morality, as tradition unanimously maintains, depends on volition, then the metaphor behind Nietzsche's punning reference to the 'exercise of the will' is relevant here. The exercise of the will is an asceticism which finds its anthropological yardstick in a human volition purged of self-concern. Asceticism can be seen as purified self-love. This learning process includes self-distancing and restraint as an inward aspect of specific development. A further essential characteristic is that of moderation as an expression of ones personality. Anyone concerned with discovering what is appropriate to him or her is also looking for a progressive equilibrium of individual potentialities, which has to be made in order for them to develop reciprocally.

Sport as a means of being human has something to do with the nature of the 'social character' (Erich Fromm) which it produces. By this I do not mean temperament, but rather, the effects of an assimilation process of the world and a socialisation process between human beings. The notion that development through sport, and ultimately sporting achievement, presupposes character is as important as the idea that it helps to produce it. It should be clear that the development of sport depends on the socio-psychological context.

According to Erich Fromm, there are two possible social orientations or tendencies: one is destructive and the other is productive. The destructive tendency may also be seen as a product – or consuming orientation, in which spiritual values become commodities viewed in terms of material desire. This tendency reduces everything that is human to the inanimate and consequently is spiritually destructive. The productive tendency, or *biophilia,* on the other hand, does not see the result of a performance as an outline or as a thing, but is interested in how the activity helps to transform the human person.[1]

II. FROM FAIRNESS TO JUSTICE[2]

On the one hand, 'fairness' comprises personal dignity: the inalienability, uniqueness and individual purposiveness of persons. On the

[1] Cf. R. FUNK, *Mut zum Menschen: Erich Fromms Denken und Werk,* Stuttgart 1978.

[2] Cf. J. RAWLS, *A Theory of Justice,* Oxford 1972; id., *The Liberal Theory of Justice,* Cambridge, Mass. 1973; O. HÖFFE, *Über John Rawls 'Theorie der Gerechtigkeit',* Frankfurt 1977; id. (ed.) *John Rawls, Gerechtigkeit als Fairness,* Freiberg 1977.

other hand, fairness also comprises traditional ideas of *aequitas,* of equity, of a balance of presuppositions, requirements and possibilities. Fair behaviour is equivalent to the one, and fair rules are equivalent to the other. Whoever wishes to be fair and just needs corresponding rules to be so. He has to make the principles of equality the basis of developing freedom, and therefore has to accept the equality of rights and obligations.

The most important practical rule of the sense of justice is the 'maximin principle' which justifies inequality only if this serves and determines the thrust of justice, so that every measure, equal or not equal, is directed to the greatest advantage (maximum) of the most disadvantaged (minimum). This criterion is unusual for us, for our society by reason of economy is accustomed to an emphatically utilitarian philosophy. A utilitarian attitude sees a measure as just if the disadvantages of certain groups can be set against the advantages of the whole. In accordance with this 'maximin' criterion, it is possible to decide whether priorities in rule interpretation, priorities in sport promotion, priorities in environmental justice, and priorities of self-control in sport are just and fair.

III. SPORT IN THE CONTEXT OF SOLIDARITY AND LIBERTY

Although the ethics of sport are most often subject to the paradigm of self-realisation, this paradigm most commonly takes place in an encounter with another person. From this viewpoint, the social dimension is ultimately an external 'imperative of avoidance'. But a constructive social emphasis would assume that sport is also thought of politically. Discussion of the so-called politicisation of sport often 'barks up the wrong tree', even though it rightly rejects inappropriate political functionalism of sport. From the ethical standpoint, however, the inappropriate politicisation of sport is not the transposition of sport into the political dimension, but the unjustifiable application of a political phenomenon to sport. Anyone who, similar to Vatican II, conceives sport as a contribution to the establishment of fraternal relations between people of all classes, countries, and races,[3] will necessarily advocate a 'political' sport. The political dimension includes on the one hand the public character of sport, and on the other hand the responsible involvement with social institutions. Sport is a public social institution. Involvement in it belongs to the realm of political ethics.

Following the principle of subsidiarity, the organisation of sport may be relative autonomous. But sport is not a societal oasis. If some societal problems connected with sport events cannot be regulated by the sporting authority itself, then the regulation by common law is necessary. Not only justice, but the principles of solidarity and liberation have to be considered here. The attainment of solidarity is a presupposition of sport itself and of involvement in sport: for access to solidarity means the simultaneous learning of restrictions and of openness. Solidarity mediates between the need for reciprocal partisanship and the drive to continually extend this option.

The concept of democracy and social liberty is important for sport to make the transition from the paradigm of an imperial developmental aid (or, as we might term it, structural promotion), to the paradigm of self-reliance in a context of liberty. Sport should be communicated politically, for it is a cultural phenomenon, but it should also be subject to emancipatory processes.

IV. SPORT WITHIN THE GLOBAL COMMON GOOD

One can see sport as a common cultural heritage of mankind. This means it is a good (even in a pre-moral sense), that corresponds to human needs and must be administered globally and under global codes. A global common good does not deny cultural differences and preferences. But the intercultural exchange of these specific prefer-

---

[3] Cf. VATICAN COUNCIL II, Past. Constitution *Gaudium et Spes*, n. 61.

ences, which are not common, is facilitated today by the mass media in such a way that the common mutual understanding of these differences has advanced so much that the experiences of strange customs now belong to the realm of familiar experiences.

The common relevance of sport is decided in practice. Perhaps there will once again be cultures in which people survive without sport and possibly live better lives without it. Nothing entitles us to assume that our cultural activity known as 'sport' is more than the result of specific social processes, the ultimate meaning of which cannot be assessed as yet. In this sense, sport is not a 'supra-temporal' but a 'historical good', which forms one of the "signs of the time" (cf. *signa temporis*, Vatican II). In fact, sport is subject to a form of historical necessity which neither society nor the individual can easily avoid but must make the best of it.

Sport is a leisure pursuit, an achievement pursuit, a mode of obedience to the drive to self-display, a means for young people to meet on a supra-national level, and a means of symbolic cultural exchange. Sport as all of these things has possible ethical implications, especially as an international youth movement and as a symbolic cultural exchange.

Sport has even been called a form of the peace movement itself. That is excessive and obscures the difference between non-moral values or commodities, and moral values which indicate the criteria for use of such commodities. For example: sport serves peace as a process of reduction of force and of inducement to social justice, when it is practised appropriately. In fact, it can be put entirely in the service of the opposite of peace: it can be used as a part of the athletic armoury of different political blocs, as a nationalistic self-enhancement, as a glorification of competitive ideology, as an aggressive potential of an individualism which employs the use of in appropriate means under the guise of acclaimed results.

Admittedly, sport politics can be tantamount to peace politics, and the pursuit of sport can adopt some of the learning processes proper to peace education. Sport as a movement to global (inter)culture is ethically relevant, but this does not happen by itself, it remains a task for all of the concerned parties (see below). This can be underlined by the negative potential which is almost on the side of the concrete praxis of sport.

V. NEGATIVE ASPECTS OF A POSTMODERN CULTURE OF SPORT

Sport as an activity that occurs within a social context does not mean that sport is one among other areas of life, but rather, that the imbuing of human beings in society with sport is a form of 'inflexional language'. Or, as Luhmann describes it, it is a form of a 'reduced complexity' in social life. It is a language which a person has to use in this particular way, even when apparently avoiding this specific area of life. Such avoidance is possible however only as a conscious refusal which is systematically and appropriately integrated into a sports context, as something 'unsporting' (which nowadays is much worse than being `unmusical`). If we accept that sport is a social context or social system in the sense of a form of reduced complexity of the world of life, it seems appropriate to consider this reduction in an environmentally 'critical' manner: that is, from the viewpoint of a 'human' environment. Then we must take the multiplicity of possible human images into account. Accordingly, I see the Christian view of humanity as an 'open concept' which comprises consistency in terms of a living tradition, and the equilibration of actual areas of human life. In light of this, the following observations seem important.

The reduction of physical activity to the cult of the body

The Fathers of the Church confronted two extreme tendencies regarding the inadequate integration of physical activity in sport in classical antiquity. On one hand there was the 'Apollonian' separation of spirit from body – the Gnostic tendency – and, on the other hand the 'Dionysian' separation of the body from spirit; that is, the body as an instrument of idolatry. The Old and New Testaments accord here with the Fathers: the games are a form of cult to idols, which Tertullian says the baptised must shun. Clement of Alexandria anticipated the judgment of the twentieth-century Church with a more nuanced opinion: "physical activity, yes; the cult of the body, no".[4] This discernment of spirits demands closer consideration.

Physical activity is reduced to the cult of the body when:

– the health of a human being is seen as a purely physical thing. Psychosomatics long ago told us that health is unattainable by isolating the body. If however the illusion is pursued that health is a purely physical functioning of the body, then physicality is an inadequate way of representing the whole human being;

– when physical appearance is confined entirely to the ideal of the athletic body. Advertising and everyday notions of appropriateness in regard to the appearance of the body, in fashion for instance, but also in normative distinctions between the sexes, confirm the ideal of a body transformed by sport. Historically speaking, this form of reductionism was not always self-evident, as Rubens' paintings show;

– when physical achievement overrides the recreational dimension. This one-sidedness of sporting achievement is more liable to harm than to promote a holistic view of physical exercise. Examples of this tendency are tennis elbow, cyclist's cramp and restraint in movement due to the excessively pronounced muscles of a weight lifter;

– when the training of the body associated with sport interrupts youthful physical development, or when sport, so to speak, exacts its price of a delayed injury which shows its negative effects in old age if not before.

---

[4] Cf. TERTULLIAN, *De spectaculis* 4 *(Selected Writings,* vol. I, Munich 1912, p. 108, I 24ff.; I 28ff. = *Bibliothek der Kirchenväter,* cd. O. Bardenhewer *et al.,* Vol. 7); CLEMENT OF ALEXANDRIA, *Paidagogos* 3, 9-10 *(cf.* A. KOCH, *Die Leibesübungen im Urteil der antiken und frühchristlichen Anthropologie,* Schorndorf 1965, pp. 84ff.); on Pius XII, *cf.* A. F. UTZ and J. F. GRONER (eds.), *Aufbau und Entfaltung des gesellschaftlichen Lebens: Soziale Summe Pius XII,* 3 vols. (Fribourg 1954 – 1961, Nos. 2016; 2044-2067; 5129-5146).

Of course these well known critical repercussions do not mean that human beings cannot live, and must not live, with these reductive features in their lives. They may do so on the condition that they observe the principles of moral integration: that is, the liberation of these reductive features from mere partial goals, from, in fact, "reductions". They also have to keep to the motto 'nothing to excess', which was Johann Michael Sailer's contribution to the debate.[5]

The social problem of physical activity resides in its instrumentalisation. Whereas before, the so-called 'games' were mere performances in which only success counted, today, participation, which is characteristic with mass sport, represents a step of progress. How magnificent to be one of the 80,000 who were allowed to take part in the New York marathon! The imbuing of life with sport is not a reduction of life to the realm of the mere physical, but rather a progressive manifestation of the cerebral in the physical: that is, the drive to achieve is ultimately located in the brain. Therefore it is scarcely surprising that in competitive sport the psychological factor is a key to success as is often the case in tennis.

The reduction of the play element by the cult of success and competition

For some time now the social symbolism of sport, even of broad-based sport, has been located not in physical activity but in the cult of success. Graf von Krokow put it this way: sport expresses the principles of industrial society belief better than that society itself.[6] Sport without something to be counted and assessed is mere play or even 'idle' art. The sporting person is the prototype of success. The achievement principle of modern society means: human equality and inequality depend on the individual, not on any inherent dignity. Each person

[5] Cf. J. M. SAILER, *Über Erziehung für Erzieher*, Munich 1809, 248-251.
[6] Cf. C. GRAF VON KROKOW, *Sport und Industriegesellschaft*, Munich 1971; W. HÄDECKE, 'Leistungssport und Leistungsgesellschaft', in: *Grenzen der Leistung*, Olten 1975, 134-146.

can be the architect of his or her own glory (consider the notion of the "pursuit of happiness" in the United States constitution).

Once the sporting maxim was "it is more important to participate than to win". Today, it would only be possible for sport to return to the level of human play if sport were pursued for the sake of play itself: that is, when playing is more important than winning. But this would mean a change in social behaviour in respect of sport. Unfortunately the general public does not think that it is more important to play than to win.

Play, in itself, is a meaningful communicative movement. That is how Vatican II sees it in *Gaudium et Spes,* citing sport as that which helps to create harmony of feeling on the level of community.[7] But the achievement culture is a reduction of communication to the level of consumption of results. The alternation of remembering and forgetting for the sportsman – producer and consumer- is characteristic of that. The modern human being has to 'train' for the play element in sport. Of course performance and play should not be forced into an absolute antithesis. The language of play must comprise the language of performance. The reductionism of performance culture in sport is directly hierarchical: that is, result-oriented performance decides the permissible elements of play.

The reduction of communication to the level of consumption

In Christian social ethics, the *ordo rerum* must remain subordinate to the *ordo personarum.* The personal element, or, in terms of social psychology, human identity, also includes subsistence or, in chronological terms, consistency and communication. In the Christian tradition the person is not an island, but realizes himself through relationships, and therefore in a communicative process. Sport is wholly a locus of communication. A series of sets of movements, which give sport its expressive power, may be interpreted as a kind of pre-linguistic or

---

[7] Cf. VATICAN COUNCIL II, Past. Constitutions *Gaudium et Spes*, n. 61.

unique linguistic communication. This is true of sport itself, above all of team sport, but also on the periphery of sport. The more sport comes under the rule of goals, success and achievement, the more one-dimensional is the possible communication of the participants, and the more it obeys the will for achievement of the industrial society or of the performance society, where everyone does his or her job.

In my opinion communication and ethics form a hermeneutical circle: that is, they mutually presuppose one another. This hermeneutical circle makes it rather difficult to distinguish between descriptive levels: between, that is, the observed communication of social mediation processes, and the evaluative level, where it is decided that communication is always desirable. Let us try the descriptive level first. The area of life known as sport represents a relatively independent system of social mediation processes, and also a relatively autonomous system of linguistic and specialist communication. If that communication is essentially performance-oriented in the sense of success and result, then communication as a form of accounting predominates. Just think of the mass media.

The counterpart of sport as a form of result-oriented communication is a result-oriented communication for the sake of sport. This is associated with acceptance behaviour. Sport-related consumer behaviour reduces social sensitivity to the result. For the critical observer, all that counts is the tension which occurs between result and performance. The imbuing of society with sport gives rise to the sport-consumer mentality, to the consumption of results. Here consumption also has a surrogate function: the possibility of living by proxy.

Compatibility with family values and other values

Sport is not necessarily in opposition to family values as both promote the need for a person to live in good relations with others whether of the same family or team. A family can insure an integrative life for children. However, often sport pushes for the individualisation of options and the pursuit of the individual's own success. In this sense, the compatibility of sport with family life may be an important litmus test for the ability of humanistic development through sports. On the other hand, sport is forming "new families" or establish familiar ties between people who otherwise live together as strangers in a pluralistic society. The integration of foreign people is one of the admired possibilities of the sport associations.

I will only take the example of the importance of environmental values like sustainability. This concerns architecture and energy as needs in sport. The question of "nature" becomes more and more a new search for adequate means and for limits of human self-creation. Sport as a mirror of the society shows the new possibilities of a culture of nature and at the same time the wide spread defects.

The question of the culture of Sunday and the other equivalent religious holidays shows an enduring conflict with sport events. But also in this case solutions are possible. They are dependent on the initiative of the involved persons and on the structures. But the Sunday is not the only question that regards religion. The relationship between sport and meditation, as well as the role of prayer in sport, needs further attention. The misuse of religious symbols as magical practices should also be further studied. Sport can also become a kind of secular religion and here the distinction of the spirit of symbols and signs must be further studied and developed also.

VI. THE COMMERCIALISATION AND MEDIA-MARKETING OF SPORT

Developments and phenomena

The collective term 'commercialisation' comprises quite different phenomena and developments, which ultimately result in a progressive interaction of economy and sport as both leisure and competition. This includes the industry of sports equipment and clothing and the construction of sports locations and the financing of sporting events, the establishment and maintenance of sport organisations and divisions, and the use of sport and sports information for publicity purposes, outside and inside the sport industry, and for the financing of promotions, premiums, compensatory payments, retainers and prize money, and the economic administration of sports manufacturers and their means of production.

In general, the economisation of politics and everyday life is a growing tendency which also means the politicisation of the economy. There is an increase in performance levels and competition. The mutual approximation of top professional sport and broad-based sport as far as performance levels and competition are concerned, means that the economisation of sport is the result of a general social development, and not an exception which can somehow be ignored. Economisation is a consequence of the growth system. The transition from quantitative growth to qualitative growth has been as little evident hitherto as the realisation of an equilibrated economy that would obey the rules of energy saving, environmental protection and just distribution. The need for economic expansion is evident everywhere in society. Science and technology develop essentially as functions of this need (cf. media development, microbiology).

The expansion of economic structures and economically conditioned behaviour into sport is, so to speak, enforced. The sporting performance which has its 'reward' in the non-economic sector (health, the discovery of identity, social communication and recognition), gives way to a form of sport which, beyond the non-economic reward, brings payments in money or other economically convertible tokens. The sport which occurs in a non- purposeful setting of mere joy in play and communication, gives way to the demands of increased turnover (publicity, marketing): that is, it is subordinate to the economic accounting of events. Leisure sport is increasingly subject to the influence of the products which, in the shape of sports equipment, sports clothing, mega stadiums, and so on, make it more effective and at the same time aid the laws of performance and competition. Anyone who falls back materially in the main areas of mass sport (skiing, tennis) cannot keep up and is no longer a recipient for non-economic 'rewards'.

The resistance of sporting organisations on the various regional, national and international levels to these developments decreased insofar as, in addition to compulsory economisation (and internationally the distinctions between social orders play no part here as long as only growth economies are concerned), the professionalization of sport increases ineluctably. This professionalization has nothing to do with the special conditions of top professional sport but has resulted from training, organisation and care in mass sport. Anyone who says 'A', that is, who is favourable to the imbuing of society with sport and to the democratisation of sporting possibilities, also has to say 'B': that is, has to take sport increasingly into account as a professional career. Naturally the consequence of this is that sport as a social service, and sport as an economic exploitation process of capital and labour, progressively reduces the partial autonomy of sport as it becomes a factor of integration in universal social developments, in which a Nobel Prize, a victory at Wimbledon and exporting a record number of motor cars have the same economic symbolic effect.

The economically and socially conditioned decrease of the partial autonomy of sport, however, which goes against the notions of a 'wholesome world' of sport that is restricted to speeches, is to be explained as a system- environment relationship. The more the selective elements of the system decrease under environmental influences, the more the system adapts to general needs and expectations, which in their turn underlie the more global form of system control. Instead of the area-specific profile, there is an increased tendency to level down at the orders of economisation, so that sport performance, the production of entertainment and scientific efficiency, and even the evangelisation of churches must obey the same rules.

Such developments can be limited by various forces, whose stability is of course exposed to the constant pressure of development: by the declaration of the partial autonomy of the sub-system in accordance with selective rules whose validity it demands for itself; by social forces which act in the name of non-economic human values and developments or obey them at least partially; by state influence, which ensures the 'freedom' of sport as much as the freedom of art and science: this is, by management of the significance of the economic valuation of products and achievements.

The commercialization of sport depends not least of all on the fact that sport *inter alia,* but increasingly, is a mass media product which is to be marketed universally almost immediately, so that sport is subject to the dual rules of its own self-regulation on the one hand and its external regulation as a media commodity on the other. The more the system of sport and the mass media system are mutually involved, the more dependent they become on one another and the greater the danger that sport communication will become the mere equivalence of two economic interest camps, without any role being accorded to consideration of 'the specific values of sport' (apart perhaps from the peripheral area of fatal collisions). The greater the economisation of sport the more the non-economic needs and values (which do not have to be ethical values in and for themselves) are forced to the periphery of sport.

Discerning spirits

Hitherto I have discussed phenomena and developments in respect of the general problem. Now I must discover some criteria for making distinctions and proceed from their basis. First of all it is necessary to establish how far the economisation of sport answers on sport goals; social needs and material needs. This would be tantamount to a search for the correct extent of a (qualitative) economisation of sport. Secondly, we have to locate precisely where the economisation of sport debouches into its commercialisation; that is, where sport becomes a commodity rather than obeying its true nature. I am using economisation here in the negative sense of commercialisation. Here the same criteria apply: the commercialisation of sport occurs when economisation takes place at the expense of sport's true ends and when economisation takes place at the cost of social needs and values.

It seems to me that these distinctions could still be made in the pre-ethical area, if the presupposition were accepted that sport possessed its own value and an associated partial autonomy; that is, sport is not allowed to masquerade in the commodity role of an economic valuation process. The distinctions become more debatable when ethical criteria for sport (representing an ethically appropriate concern with the values of sport) are to be brought into the context of universal socio-ethical notions (of, say, Christian social teaching) for the discernment of spirits.

Then it is a question (in the third instance) not only of the restriction of commercialisation within the setting of a compulsory economisation, but of the limitation of *homo oeconomicus* by means of a holistic conception of human beings pure and simple. That requires the introduction of positive criteria: a non-economic form of human dignity; the revaluation of non-economic needs and corresponding value orientations or basic attitudes; the proposal not only of personal but of structural alternatives to the developments described. The use of such criteria is certainly possible only in discussions with experts from other disciplines or with some other form of practical experience. In the following, therefore, I shall mention only a few examples which might help to explain the relevant criteria more effectively.

Some examples of an appropriate economisation of sport

Aims of sport are, for instance, exercise, training in movement, pleasure in achievement, personal relations and social recognition. Economic means and economically responsible planning are necessary to promote these goals. In so far as free economic forces co-operate in the promotion of these goals while furthering their own interests, their efficiency must also be assessed in regard to these aims.

Social needs are, for instance, help for the socially disadvantaged (*e.g.* sport for the handicapped, structural aid to rural areas or new urban housing projects) and an absence of information. Here too it is possible to accommodate particular economic interests (all the more so if work can also be provided). Here it is a question of balancing the ends with the means.

Material demands include, for instance, more professionalism in training, recreation and organisation. Here, in addition to balancing ends against means, it is also a matter of supporting, influencing, and balancing these same interests.

Some examples of an inappropriate economisation of sport

At the expense of sporting goals and aims: if, instead of physical exercise, play, and achievement, the main concern is with the entertainment of spectators; if direct human contact is lost in favour of the isolation of individual performances; if the formation of a sports elite loses contact with the basis; if the commercialisation of the promotion of achievement uses impermissible means (stress and damage to health; the use of questionable drugs); if sports medicine becomes more important than training; and so on.

At the expense of social needs and valuations: if the maintenance and origin of other leisure and cultural values are impaired; if the promotion of sport in events and broadcasts leads to competition with other needs (care for the family, personal interests); if industrial concerns promote sport but omit to humanise the workplace; if sport and care for the environment are made to compete, and so forth.

By altering the degree of material necessity: if it is only the market value of performance in sport seen as a commodity which determines its reward instead of the achievement itself, and the appropriate needs of the sports person; if the sports organisation, bureaucracy, and information function solely in accordance with commercial demands; if professionalization sees its task as primarily one of serving the interests of competitive achievement and not as the increase of other sporting goals; in short: if commerce decides the aims of sport instead of the other way round.

VII. Criteria that favours human dignity

Since human dignity is not decided by economic ends (even though it requires economic means), the following criteria have to be observed: human self-determination *(e.g.* should parents and educators mark out children as future sportsmen and sportswomen?); fundamental human needs (in addition to basic physiological needs, the need for personal relations, social recognition, and meaning: should success in sport downgrade superior needs?); individual and social rights *(e.g.* the right to an appropriate education, to the opportunity to choose one's vocation, to work as a fundamental principle of self-realisation, and so on); respect for humanity dignity as a self-explanatory goal in human relations (how far does commercialization threaten human relations, inasmuch as one's fellow human being becomes no more than a means to winning?).

Value-orientation and basic attitudes: if sport is to help make possible a 'productive' human orientation (in contrast to a 'destructive' orientation), then the following criteria have to be observed: justice as fairness; the capacity for self-restriction; the promotion of life and environmental justice; the potentiality of peace.[8] Such values can only be reached if human needs remain uncommercialized.

Structural alternatives: here it is a matter of establishing due proportions between the relevant criterion, the means used, and the goals of human success. This is achieved, not by appealing solely to the individual athlete who is involved, but rather, as a broad campaign that promotes the structural conditions for 'rational' sports persons.

Such considerations come to the forefront in utopias, such as an anti- or alternative Olympics. Perhaps there are less complicated instances. Unfortunately a more detailed account is beyond my competence. Nevertheless I can envisage a reduction of the unilateralism

---

[8] Cf. D. Mieth, *Die neuen Tugenden*, Düsseldorf 1984, 107-141.

of sport by a constant introduction of new areas of competition. The foregoing are merely experimental illustrations of the relevant criteria. The moral theologian can do no more than suggest possible criteria; he cannot provide actual solutions.

VIII. THE ETHICAL FOUNDATION OF THE SOCIAL BAN AGAINST DOPING[9]

In spite of the complexity of the doping phenomenon, it is clear that the debate must not be reduced to only two factors: health protection and unfair performance enhancement. While health and fairness are important – and they remain core values of sport (see below) – they must also be seen in the context of, and in conflict with, other values; the autonomy of the mature sportsman or woman, exceeding previous limits of performance and success – faster, further, higher than before – and the feelings associated with tension in extreme situations. However, there are two very cogent ethical arguments which consider doping to be reprehensible from various points of view that I will now consider.

The contract argument

According to this, the sportsperson has a contract with the sports organisations in participating in his sport, competitions and training, which requires him to adhere to certain rules, even if, in certain cases, these rules may appear to be questionable, wrong or unfounded. Athletes entrust the association with this important task of drawing up lists of banned substances for performance enhancement, reduction of strain, regeneration etc., which they implicitly understand or explicitly express (e.g. in the Olympic oath). They therefore also agree with

---

[9] Cf. the Opinion on Doping of the EGE (European Group on Ethics in the Sciences and in the New Technologies) of 2000, found in a link on the webpage of the European Union: http://europa.eu.int/comm/european_group_ethics/secret_en.htm

penalties if they contravene the agreement. Athletes can make this clear through a personal oath. The agreement gives them rights as well as obligations.

The argument of the inconsistency of values, rights and obligations

This argument is taken up by sport itself, and by society, which wants sport to set an example of excellence. Sport cannot, on the one hand, claim such values, rights and obligations in theory, and on the other negate them in practice. The phenomena of commercialisation, media domination and medicalization that we have referred to are dependent on a kind of added value resulting from them to profit by them. Sport, which also gains from this, is subject to the obligation to maintain these values, rights and obligations which it demands and claims for itself. In fact its credibility depends upon it. Hypocrisy would compromise this social contract with sport.

IX. The social contract with sport

The social contract with sport concerns the values which are inherent to sport and explain its prestige and power of attraction; the rights which active and passive participants in sport can demand to exercise; and the obligations of mutual solidarity which bind sport and a democratic society.

The values or assets on which sport is based and whose realisation is ethically relevant or, in part, ethically feasible are, in contrast to those of active participants- namely health, fitness, *joie de vivre,* discipline, team spirit and training opportunities- cultural values such as travel, languages, leisure etc. In relation to other participants these values are friendship, fairness, cultural integration, recognition of "otherness", consideration for others, etc. In relation to the social status of sport, these values are setting examples in the achievement-oriented society and the solidarity-oriented society alike, cultural and training functions, integration of foreigners, the moral dimension of developments in society and their manifestations, etc.

The rights embodied in sport are self-development and self-awareness together with a voluntary commitment to the values acknowledged through participation in sport. These include: the right to the inviolability of one's own body, and to develop it according to personality and gender; the right not to be exploited; the protection of vulnerable groups (e.g. sport for the disabled); equality of access, limited only by talent and achievement and non-discriminatory; the right not to be deceived or led astray; the right to a reasonable balance between risks and success; the right not to be harmed by others (trainers, competitors, doctors, associations, media, public); the right of active participants to take part in decision-making; and the right to share in the resources created by sport, etc.

The obligations of solidarity important to sport include preventive measures to protect the sporting nature of sport and its associated values; appropriate cultural assistance, or, where necessary, the withdrawal of such assistance; a legal framework based on subsidiarity; consideration of the social, ecological and media environment; protective measures for active and passive participants in sport; obligations of solidarity between active participants; obligations of solidarity on the part of the active participants as regards legitimate expectations.

Sports culture also involves a recipient's ethic. If the media and the public close their eyes to negative phenomena to maintain an idealised image, they invalidate their demand for trust. Instead of a covenant between society and a sport based on values, rights and obligations, there is only a sport as entertainment without responsibility.

Opportunities and resources for renewal in sport

Edio Costantini*

Sport has spread worldwide to an extraordinary degree, and across the years it has acquired increasing importance in the lives of people of every age and social status. Its worldwide character is due to its exceptional variety. For there are many different ways of understanding, organising and practising sport. Unfortunately, however, the many ways in which sports are practised today are not always designed for the comprehensive development of the human person, nor do they always build a better society, which is what the philosophy of sport claims for it.

Looking at the world of sport we cannot fail to see a number of alarming tendencies emerging, driven by the dominant culture, such as the ruthless selection of the fittest, the alienation of athletes as persons, turning them into clients or commodities whose only purpose is to generate the maximum profit, the indiscriminate use of drugs to improve competitive performance, the widening gap between élite sport and grassroots sport which is being increasingly emphasised by globalisation, the growing readiness to see sport merely in terms of political and financial interests, and the subservience of sport to the rationale of economic might. All this is further magnified by the spiralling development of the mass media that project behavioural models based on egotism, individualism, consumerism and the exploitation

* A native of the Marche region (Italy), where he grew up in *Centro Sportivo Italiano*, (CSI) and Catholic Action, in 1991 Edio Costantini was appointed National Secretary of the CSI, which, since 2000, he has been the President. CSI was established in 1944 as a Catholic Action initiative to promote sport as an educational instrument and a means of creating social cohesion, based on the Christian vision of man. CSI originally grew up around the parish "oratorio" clubs, but was not limited to Catholic sports associations alone. Today, CSI has some 850,000 at the members in 13,000 clubs.

45

of the human person. Today's situation is alarming for those concerned about promoting a sport that is accessible to everyone, educational in scope, and founded upon justice and solidarity.

In the light of these issues, sports associations, particularly Catholic associations, cannot be content with merely being present in the world of sport, but they must affirm their specific identity, placing themselves at the service of men and women, and bringing out the real priorities in competitive sport. Our athletes cannot be relegated to being "consumers" of sport alone. Physical exercise is certainly of fundamental importance, but it is not the sole aspect. The first, and the most important, purpose of sport must be to foster the advancement of the person who practises it.

For we must never forget that among the "historic" purposes of sport – the harmonious development of the body, socialisation, the protection of health – its educational function was always essential, a function which is not taken into account today. And yet it is obvious that it is an indispensable element, considering the space that sport occupies in the lives of young people today. Any sport which is not concerned with the formation of tomorrow's human capital loses the greatest part of its meaning and social value.

I. The risk of emptying sport of the ethical dimension

The deterioration of the sports ethos is at the heart of he demise of the educational function of support. The fact that sport runs the risk of losing an ethical soul is known to all, and was emphasised several times, in quite forthright language, by John Paul II during his pontificate. For sport is not immune to the process through which contemporary societies are being emptied of their ethical dimension, and it also suffers from fads and fashions with no human substance or values, based on selfishness, competition pushed to extremes, and commercialisation.

In this connection, John Paul II urged sports associations to commit themselves to ensuring that their mission is not merely to promote competition but also to contribute to "responding to the deep-seated questions that the new generations are asking regarding the meaning of life, its orientation and its purpose".[1] These words provide the key to interpreting the present moment. We must come to terms with the widespread process of de-Christianisation, and a weak, lax and permissive educational culture: the family, the school, and parishes are finding it difficult to renew their proposals and the instruments at their disposal. The materialistic and individualistic culture that has been imposed in recent years is tending to rob the human soul of the hope of eternity, dazzling us with promises of illusory happiness linked to consumption, and causing people to lose the sense of striving, achieving and sacrificing for a goal.

Against this background, Catholic sports associations must be committed to bearing witness to the Christian values that sport promotes, to act as a critical conscience, to openly voice opposition to the negative things which are affecting the practice of sport, and make a positive impact in those *forums* that are responsible for promoting and enhancing the social function of sport. This demands not only a realistic grasp of the present situation in order to discern between what is truly "essential" and what is purely technical or organisational, but also a prophetic interpretation. The later makes one capable of accepting change, combining the new and the old, and of successfully appraising the signs of crisis that are becoming increasingly evident today, and are threatening the ethical roots of sport itself.

We are therefore being called to a great mobilisation in order to liberate sport from all these economic, political and ideological constraints that have robbed it of meaning. We are being called to ensure that, before anything else, the good of the person and the non-negotiable value of human life is upheld.

---

[1] JOHN PAUL II, *Address to members of the Italian Sports Centre: Called to be Christ's witnesses in Sport* "L'Osservatore Romano" Weekly English Edition, n. 28 July 14, 2004, 3.

II. The educational power of sport

The Holy Father, Benedict XVI, in his address to the young people in Cologne for World Youth Day, said that said that "in their hearts, people always and everywhere have somehow expected a change, a transformation of the world".[2] The central act of this change that can renew the world, he said, is the substantial transformation that was accomplished at the Last Supper, by making the bread into his body and the wine into his blood, when violence was transformed into love, and death into life". This victory of love over hatred is described by Benedict XVI as like "inducing nuclear fission" into the very heart of being, which is capable of "triggering a series of transformations that little by little will change the world".[3] These are words that have a great deal to say to the world of sport, which certainly needs great transformations, considering the confusion which reigns there, and the loss of quality and the loss of meaning from which it is currently suffering.

What is most regrettable is the fact that sport is no longer being put forward as a means of forming new generations, but is solely for economic interests, and for laying on a public spectacle, thereby reneging on its most ancient values and failing to honour its responsibilities to contemporary society.

But this must not discourage us. For there are still men and women who are committed to bringing about a real rebirth of sport, to restore to it its original value and to re-humanise it. The renewal of sport is possible, but it depends on us, and on how far we are able to allow that intimate explosion of good, to which the Holy Father referred, to take its course and deploy its capacity to influence everything that is around it, and to transform lives.

The real challenge that sport has to face today is educational in

---

[2] Benedict XVI, *Homily, Holy Mass at Marienfeld Esplanade (Cologne): Entering the 'hour'*, "L'Osservatore Romano" Weekly English Edition, n. 34, August 24, 2005, 11.
[3] *Ibid.*

character. One of the emergencies in contemporary society is certainly the need to attract young people away from "nothingness", banalities, and the mediocrity on which boredom, loneliness and crises feed. I believe, in this regard, that despite all the problems I have just mentioned, sport still has so much to offer young people.

Our commitment – the commitment of everyone engaged in the sports world, sports officials and managers – must be to promote sporting, cultural and recreational activities that involve the largest possible number of young people, and that can give them not only the opportunity to devote themselves to one particular sport, but something even more precious still: the source of hope that will not let them down, because it is precisely in their youthful years when our words and actions can inspire them to find meaning for their lives.

Every young person yearns for happiness, and it is precisely in this yearning that we find the roots of the educational value of sport. Sport, which entails trials and sacrifices, thrills and disappointments, goals to be reached and to renew continuously, is a great school for living. Training for sport can therefore become the easiest and the most direct way of training for life.

III. RESTORING A FACE AND A SOUL TO SPORT

The International Convention that was held on the eve of the Jubilee for Sports People in 2000 addressed a very interesting theme, "The face and soul of sport". I think that, particularly today, the face and the soul of sport do not often coincide. There is a great discrepancy between the widespread appeal to noble values of sport with the occasions of great sporting events, and the absence of these values in sport on a daily basis. One often hears it claimed, for example, that the Olympic ideals foster tolerance, brotherhood and peace between peoples. In the name of these ideals Olympic truces are often invoked to suspend wars and armed conflicts throughout the duration of the Olympics. This is certainly admirable. However, sport would make the argument much more credible if it were the first to declare its readiness to suspend sport competitions as a means of forcefully drawing public attention to the arguments in favour of peace.

Yet, we have to confront a world of sport that is filled with contradictions and has little or no powerful ideals or drive for renewal. While aware of these contradictions and this discrepancy between the values sport proclaims and the values it actually practises, between its public face and its private soul, those engaged in the world of sport must commit themselves to recuperating a sport that can play an effective role in meeting today's needs.

Sport has need of a soul which is capable of speaking to young people about eternal ideals. It has need of a face that reflects these ideals. This is the task that falls to everyone and which can certainly be developed from the grass roots upwards. In order to renew sport and enable it to rediscover its true nature it is certainly not necessary to wait for leading sports associations and institutions to implement improvement policies of their own. Sport possesses its own resources, on which all can draw, to overcome risks and ambiguities, and become truly a vehicle of values, and a sphere for fostering culture, humanity and civility.

IV. The pillars of a sport that educates

What can be done then, to enable sport to rediscover coherent ideals with a solid ethos, and to become a meaningful tool that can be used by individuals and societies, and thereby "promote sports which can create the condition of a life rich in hope"?[4] I believe that there are three pillars on which our actions have to be based: 1) the non-negotiable value of the human person; 2) the value of volunteerism in sport; 3) the value of sports associations.

---

[4] John Paul II, *Address to Conference of Sports and Ethics: Sports can be viewed as a service to mankind.* "L'Osservatore Romano" Weekly English Edition, n. 2, January 8, 1990, 5.

The nonnegotiable value of the human person

In his address to participants of the Congress on Sport and Ethics, held by the Italian Bishops Conference in 1989, John Paul II emphasised the fact that "the ethical conditions of the person in sports and the various situations of athletic organization also need a reference to the relativity of sport in regard to the primacy of the person, thus emphasizing the subsidiary role of sports in God's creative plan".[5] Rehumanising sport and restoring its dignity and value, making it a means of meeting deep-seated human needs, is therefore only possible if the human person is the centrepiece of any reflection on sport. For the practice of sport, intended as a means of enabling those who practise it to develop and grow, encourages them to undertake a daily commitment to practise and spread the values of friendship, fellowship, solidarity and peace, and hence contribute towards the coming of that "civilisation of love", the goal for which John Paul II encouraged us to strive. On another occasion he observed that "the potential of sport makes it a significant vehicle for the overall development of the person and a very useful element in building a more human society".[6] We must therefore encourage the definition of sport that is capable of offering a specific cultural and educational project, and whose constant benchmark is the integral development of the person.

The value of volunteerism

We have already said that sport is educational when certain conditions are met, and above all if those working in the world of sport truly desire to make it educational. The first condition for those who work as volunteers in youth sports, is that they have a passion for education,

---

[5] *Ibid.*

[6] JOHN PAUL II, *Address to the International Convention on Sport during the Jubilee: Sport can help to build civil society*, "L'Osservatore Romano" Weekly English Edition, n. 46, November 15, 2000, 9.

which requires true concern for the lives of those entrusted to their care, despite the difficulties this entails. This passion for education is the unique aspect that characterizes voluntary youth sports. It is also the fundamental resource within sport and distinguishes mere "service providers" from true "educators", who in the latter case, by virtue of their commitment, have the determination and the motivation to swim against the tide, to address difficult situations. They are also a sign of hope within sport, through sport and for sport.

In their critical formative years, young people feel the need to create their own life project, to feel useful in society, and to find solid models from which to take their inspiration. This is made all the more difficult today by the many social changes taking place. Hence the urgent need for sport educators who are capable of being much more than teachers of techniques or trainers of physical skills. They must also know how to make these young people feel accepted, direct them, and accompany them along their path, thus giving them hope. In fact, by "doing things together", which is typical of education, they can foster the full development of young men and women, and strengthen their self-esteem, identity, and hence their autonomy. Only the type of sport that knows how to educate people in the ethical foundations of life – personal responsibility, the value of relating to others, and solidarity – can give young people the certainties they need, showing them that the path of values and ideals is the one that is right for them, in order to build up their own identity and reach out to the needs of others.

The value of sports associations

In most European countries the social fabric has been gradually unravelling for several decades, and the effects for the youth of today –marginalisation, the spread of drug addiction and urban violence- are things with which we have become all too familiar. In such a weak social environment from the point of view of educational and training opportunities, sports associations can certainly make a valuable contribution to civil society because they have the appropriate means of encouraging the implementation of youth programs and policies, designed to establish strong individual and group identities and to develop the ability to relate, and to foster inclusion. Some associations even design and implement national and international networks capable of training young people, and supporting the work of families and educational agencies, and of disseminating a culture of integration between countries in order to solve the problems raised by immigration.

It is certainly possible to achieve these objectives through the work of sports clubs and associations where the formative value of sport can be deployed to the full, because, in addition to being places for practising sport, they also offer guidance and counselling, listening, community, and rehabilitation. If these clubs are to make definitive responses to today's demands they have to be configured not only as sports services providers, but as important pathways of life, geared to fundamental values. Dynamic sports clubs are therefore needed, that are ever ready to listen to the human and educational needs in their localities, open to cooperation with other educational bodies (families, schools, parishes...) and ready to take in everyone, particularly those in the greatest need of support for their formation and education. The activities of these clubs must be authentic experiences of life, hinging essentially around the need to help every athlete to give the best of themselves whether in training or competition, or at school, in a group, or at home.

V. Conclusions

Sport is certainly not a panacea for all the ills of today's disturbed world, and in particular the world of youth. But there is no doubt that it is an extremely popular human activity that can be advantageous in establishing role models and very usefully influence the structuring of personalities and behavioural models. For practising sport is an important means of human and social development, if it forms part of a specific and clearly defined educational context, because it enables individuals to acquire essential qualities and attitudes in life, such as self-knowledge, self-control, autonomy, the ability to compete, cooperate and accept sacrifices to achieve a purpose, and to accept both victory and defeat with good grace.

Educationists all agree that the practice of sport is very important for young people, because it obliges boys and girls to actively employ their psychophysical energies to act purposefully, to establish very close relationships with their contemporaries, and to structure their free time. All these are skills which, if acquired in their adolescence in a sports environment, are useful to people of all ages and in every sphere of life.

In conclusion, I should like to share with you my deep desire for this seminar to be, as John Paul II said at the Jubilee of Sports People, "an opportunity to find new creative and motivating zeal, so that sport, without losing its true nature, can answer the needs of our time: sport that... frees young people from the snares of apathy and indifference, and arouses a healthy sense of competition in them;... sport which contributes to the love of life, teaches sacrifice, respect and responsibility, leading to the full development of every human person".[7]

---

[7] JOHN PAUL II, *Homily at the Jubilee for the World of Sport: Even the greatest champions need Christ,* "L'Osservatore Romano" Weekly English Edition, n. 44, November 1, 2000, 1.

Sport as viewed from the Church's Magisterium

CARLO MAZZA*

As a unique, conscious human activity that engages the entire
person through a series of unified, and structured, bodily gestures that test one's individual physical abilities, sport has drawn the
attention of the Church. In fact, sport, as an expression of a synchro-
nized action of freedom, will, emotion, and corporality, manifests a
great human undertaking and reveals certain characteristics of the
human person as a creature who longs to transcend the very limits of
his own being.

Church and sport: a relationship of many years

The Church, "expert in humanity" – according to the well noted
phrase of Paul VI – looks benevolently upon sport with its individual,
social and cultural dimensions, giving each one of these a positive eval-
uation. The Church recognizes the role that sport can play in perfecting the human person with its potential to moderate human instinct
and its capacity to gather people together towards a common goal,
promoting fellowship, solidarity, and peace through its universal
appeal and ability to draw people from different cultures and backgrounds together in friendly competition.

This vast horizon of positive opportunities confers on sport a generous yield, especially when it is a human action carried out with

---

* Msgr. Carlo Mazza is a priest originally from the diocese of Bergamo, Italy. Since
1988, he has been the head of the office for the pastoral ministry of Leisure, tourism, and
sport of the Italian Bishops Conference, which was one of the first to institute such a
national office. In addition to compiling numerous pastoral documents on sport, Msgr.
Mazza has also been the chaplain to the Italian Olympic team since 1988.

respect for the rules and in a healthy competitive spirit. These sound results are complemented by an enrichment of the person and of society, in an experience of self satisfaction as well as the joy of community. In order to have an immediate panorama of the vast and complex world of sport today, we can borrow from the French author, Bernard Jeu. According to him, traces of all aspects of reality are to be found in sport: the aesthetic aspect (because sport is observed); the technical aspect (because sport is learned); the commercial aspect (because sport is sold as a good and used to sell many other goods); the political aspect (because sport exalts cities and nations, while at the same time it can cross boundaries and frontiers); the medical aspect (because it implies the exercise of the body); the legal aspect (because without universal rules, competition is not possible); the religious aspect (because it has religious roots and – as some claim – has become a modern religion).[1]

In this perspective, sport appears as something all encompassing, universal, and of immense cultural resonance with respect to many other human activities. In fact, as sport grows in popularity, in practice, and in media presence, it is becoming a point of convergence for diverse interests, an attractive professional field of interest, a multidisciplinary school of different ways of thought, a huge business network, and a phenomenon of our epoch. Furthermore, through its constant expansion, sport it cuts across and permeates significant sectors of individual and social life, soliciting and even manipulating new interests, under numerous aspects, that were not present in the original and neutral state of athletic activity.

Before this imposing phenomenon of modern sport, the Church has not been afraid of confronting "in a sporting way" – if I may use such a term – this great challenge. The Church has formulated an original reflection with regard to sport, and has encouraged its proper practice, first in the area of education within the Church, and later within the greater realm of civil society.

---

[1] Cf. B. JEU, *Le sport, la mort, la violence*, PUF, Paris 1976.

It should be immediately noted here that the Church's "way of thinking" regarding sport, which began in an initial form and gradually developed with greater intensity and clarity, has come about by the wise intuition and the acute sensibility of the supreme pontiffs, independently of their personal involvement in sports or their predisposition for sporting activity.

In fact, the pontiffs throughout the 20th century have shown a special interest in sport, even if some of their discourses were only for a specific occasion. These discourses manifest an enlightened perception of the evident value that sport plays within a modern culture that has been shaped by rapid change in the wake of the industrial revolution and the subsequent changes in the customs and lifestyles of the masses, as well as the frantic quest by man to affirm his own subjectivity and individual freedom.

Regarding the sporting phenomena, the pontiffs have outlined a unique synthesis that, at first glance, does not seem to arise from any one school of thought. It is founded upon and guided by principles of the moral order pertaining to the physical well being and the supernatural purpose of the human person. They have noted the physical, psychological, and spiritual benefits that come from the practice of sport, while, at the same time, they have underlined the risks and related dangers that derive from serious distortions of fundamental ethical norms.

Through the years, a sort of Church "doctrine" regarding sport has been emerging little by little, which is capable of interpreting sporting phenomena, in the light of the faith, and in connection to the general ethical principles of the natural and supernatural order. Yet, this set of teachings has never been developed to the point of reaching a mature and organic synthesis in an official Church document.[2]

---

[2] It is interesting to note that the pontiffs of the 20th century gave over *200* discourses (from simple greetings, to more elaborate speeches) that can be divided among them in this way: Pius X, *3*; Benedict XV, *1*; Pius XI, *5*; Pius XII, *20*; John XXIII, *9*; Paul VI, *35*; John Paul II, *120*. A comprehensive collection of these messages, as well as a systematic and rigorous study is needed.

Consequently, in the pontifical teachings of the 20th century from Pius X to John Paul II, and most recently with Pope Benedict XVI, we can find a homogenous and progressive "corpus" of sporting discourses, to which new content regarding the ethical, the cultural, and the practice of sport, continue to be added, with their emphasis on one theme or another, depending on the particular audience being addressed and their social-cultural context.[3]

A preliminary analysis of these papal texts reveals no immediate or explicit intention to develop an organic formulation of the thought of the Church regarding sport in a systematic way. In fact, each pontifical intervention was made within a particular ecclesial context, and determined in great part by the specific characteristics of the audience, and often tied to a particular circumstance or the celebration of a particular event or activity within the Church or within society as a whole. Consequently, these exterior factors have determined the quality of these pontifical addresses, in as much as they were restricted by time from fully developing a theme, or often limited to essential or practical indications, frequently sparse in biblical or theological references, and tailored to the audience being addressed.

For the present task at hand, that of presenting a vision of sport in the light of the Magisterium of the Church, I want to mention one word about the method I will employ. Instead of sticking to a strictly diachronic progression, I will proceed synchronically. That is, instead of tracing the development of the Magisterium of the Church in a historical way, I prefer to order this development according to the major themes of general hermeneutic interest. This choice will favour a more synthetic understanding of the essential points of the "thought" of the

---

[3] Some informal "collections" of these Papal discourses in Italian were published by the following: G. PINTO, *Lo sport negli insegnamenti pontifici da Pio X a Paolo VI*, AVE, Roma 1964; E. DE PANFILIS, *Tempo libero, turismo e sport: la risposta della Chiesa*, vol. 1-2, Libreria Gregoriana, Padova 1986; C. RINALDI, *Giovanni Paolo II e lo sport*, Movimento Sportivo Popolare Europeo, Roma 1990; G.B. GANDOLFO-L. VASSALLO (ed.), *Lo sport nei documenti pontifici*, La Scuola, Brescia 1994.

pontiffs, over and above the precise historic moment in which each pontifical discourse was delivered.[4]

A new direction for sport in light of the council

This method should not prevent us from seeing how a certain turning point came about in this development, even if the substance of the papal teaching maintained its overall continuity. We can see this in the wake of the intense theological and pastoral development of the Second Vatican Council. It was there, within the broader context of the relationship between the Church and the world, that the Church examined the sporting phenomenon in order to determine the emerging factors produced by these cultural changes. The Council reflected on the urgent need for spiritual development of trainers and athletes. It discussed the manifestations of those things that degrade sport, such as violence, doping, and commercialization. These are complex phenomena, fruit of an osmosis between sport and society, that require further reflection and study.

The Council marked a turning point and revealed a wider vision on the part of the Church towards sports. The perspective of the Council evaluates the new complexities of sport today with all of its multifaceted elements which can no longer be contained by the explicit canons of scholasticism due to their complexity and breadth. Sport is now a global reality that intertwines a countless number of social, economic, and even medical-pharmaceutical components. It is now enhanced by technology, and has made its triumphal entry into the field of television.

Because of this, the world of sport is now seen in a new perspec-

---

[4] It should be noted that the commentaries about sport in the last century have been made essentially by the Papal Magisterium. A parallel commentary cannot be found on the part of the individual Bishops. It is only recently that the Italian Bishop's Conference has published a pastoral document on *"Sport and Christian life"* (1995) that followed an analogous document by the Polish Bishop's Conference (1991).

tive. The player, once the only protagonist, is now subjected to the contradictions that these external factors impose on sport, such as the massive investments of sponsors, the embellishment of the game in order to appeal to the mass of spectators, or the media driven time constraints of the game itself. The end result is that the player himself often feels like a prisoner in his own game.

Both the athlete and his profession are undergoing an anthropological and aesthetical metamorphosis. Little by little, his former status as a player – one who once trained anonymously – has been converted into that of the superstar of the stadium and a media celebrity. The athlete has become a hero, honored and worshipped as the unique object of the spasmodic outbursts of the crowds of fans who hold him up as if he were a mythic figure to imitate. Drawing upon not only his personal success, but also on the huge success of this business, the athlete has become a "new product" subject to the laws of consumer consumption. Sophisticated and attractive as an elite public celebrity, the athlete is always "in form" and continually in the spotlight.

As the popularity of sport increases its influence over the masses, the attraction of its success tends to turn sport into a gimmick, a mere pretence that can easily draw millions of people whether spectators, consumers, or venders, who, without any critical eye, swallow this up in a process that is ever more void of any real significance or value.

During the work of the Council, and in particular when drawing up the pastoral constitution *Gaudium et spes*, the topic of sport entered the discussion for the first time.[5] The debate concluded with the decision to incorporate this topic into paragraph 61 of the chapter entitled, "The proper development of culture". In this number, the Council recognized that "physical exercise and sport help to create harmony of feeling even on the level of the community as well as foster friendly relations between men of all classes, countries, and races".[6]

---

[5] See A. LATTUADA, *Lo sport nel magistero della Chiesa*, in C. MAZZA (ed.) "Fede e sport. Fondamenti, contesti, proposte pastorali", Piemme, Casale Monferrto 1994, 67-68.

[6] VATICAN COUNCIL II, Pastoral Constitution *Gaudium et spes*, n. 61.

This fact assumes historical relevance and reveals a new approach as it situates sport among those activities which are at the very heart of a culture. This placement, while offering sport unexpected attention, at the same time enabled a more precise, dynamic and critical interpretation of it that is in step with the rapid changes of the time. In this way, the new horizon opened by the Council led the Church right into the middle of the phenomenon of sport, together with its potential for good as well as its contradictions, facilitating a necessary dialogue, as well as an even more necessary "evangelisation" of this "new areopagus".

The Church's genuine interest in sport

Before this perspective, it is good to briefly pause to ask why the Church was, and continues to be concerned about sport. Certainly it is not for its own sporting interest or any other social interest. The Church is above all concerned about the human person: the profound destiny of humanity and the mission of revealing to all people the only Saviour, Jesus Christ and the identification with his way of life as the path to salvation.

With the specific reference made to the "sports person" and to "sporting activity", the Church has expressed a wise and convincing theological and spiritual doctrine that overcomes the spiritual or material dualism that have often impeded an objective and comprehensive understanding of sport. At the same time, the Church provides concrete points of application regarding its practice.

The inquiry about the ultimate meaning of sport for the Church was expressly made by Pius XII. In an address to Roman athletes, Pius XII applied St. Paul's exhortation, "Whether you eat or drink, whatever it is that you do, do it all for the glory of God" (*1 Cor* 10:31) to all physical activity and this consequently includes sport. In fact he boldly exclaims: "How can the Church not be interested in sport?"[7] By this

---

[7] PIUS XII, *Address to Roman Athletes,* May 20, 1945. English translation found in R. FEENEY, *A Catholic Perspective: Physical Exercise and Sport*, Aquinas Press, Virginia 1995, 28. Original Italian text found in "Discorsi e radiomessaggi di Pio XII" VII (1945), 56.

rhetorical question he intended to dispel the lurking opinions that rejected the idea that the Church could have any interest whatsoever in the practice of sport.

With this point well established, it can then be more readily stated that the Church "sees in sport a gymnasium of the spirit, a means to exercise moral education; and because of this it admires, approves, and encourages the practice of sport in its various forms, that of youth sports whose practice harmonically develops the body in its physical potential, as well as the competitive sport".[8] The Church's interest, then, is directed to man and the temporal dimension of his life. Motivated by a genuine care for the person, in both his or her physical and spiritual well-being, the Church also has concern for sport in as much as it is "ordered to the intellectual and moral perfection of the soul".[9]

To better understand the reason behind the Church's interest for sport, we will take a look at some of the most salient moments in which the Church has manifested this attention. It is not the mere question of "what does the Church think about sport", as if the Church were simply a public opinion agency. No. Rather, the question must be "how does the Church realize her mission in sport?" in as much as the Church as a community of witnesses of the Risen Christ announces the message of salvation even within the world of sport.

The goal of sport is the good of the person

One of the continual themes throughout the teaching of the Church regarding sport is the expression of utmost concern in safeguarding the integrity of the human person. This is a line of thought that is rooted in Christian anthropology and the social doctrine of the

---

[8] PAUL VI, *Address to cyclists of Giro d'Italia*, May 30, 1964 [our translation]. Original Italian text can be found in G.B. GANDOLFO-L. VASSALLO (editors), *Lo sport nei documenti pontifici*, La Scuola, Brescia 1994, 151.

[9] PIUS XII, *Address to the Italian Sports Centre*, October 9, 1955 [our translation]. Original Italian text in "Discorsi e radiomessaggi di Pio XII" XVII (1955), 283.

Church, especially the principles of subsidiarity and solidarity. In light of the inalienable value of the dignity and integrity of the person as a unity of body and soul, the Church asks sport not only to respect the identity of the person, but also to allow the individual to develop his or her full potential with regard to God's plan for his or her life.

In sport, the human body is the "instrument"; the body is not an end in itself. Pius XII clarifies this in a noted discourse on the four purposes of sport, where he states: "sport and gymnastics have, as their immediate purposes, that of the education, development, and strengthening of the body in its constitution and power of movement. As their more remote purpose, you have the use made, by the soul, of the body so prepared, for the development of the interior or exterior life of the person; as their still deeper purpose, that of contributing to its perfection; and lastly, there is the supreme purpose of man as man, the goal common to every form of human activity –that of bringing man closer to God".[10]

Outlining these fundamental "ends" enables one to better determine sport's global value for the Church. These four purposes of sport constitute an essential nucleus that can be understood in light of an underlying "theology of the body". In fact, it is the theological and spiritual elaboration of this theme that engages a dynamic hermeneutic that draws from divine Revelation. From this we can deduce that the true theological motivation is founded on a Christian anthropology that is not in anyway juxtaposed to the original plan of God the Creator, but rather, substantially linked to it.

As Pius XII also noted: "The human body is, in its own right, God's masterpiece in the order of visible creation. The Lord has intended that it should flourish here below and enjoy immortality in the glory of heaven. He has linked it to spirit in the unity of the human nature, to give to the soul a taste of the enchantment of the works of

---

[10] Pius XII, *Address to participants of the Italian National Scientific Congress for Sport and Physical Education*, November 8, 1952. English translation from R. Feeney, *A Catholic Perspective: Physical Exercise and Sport*, Aquinas Press, Virginia 1995, 45.

God's hands, to help it to see the Creator of them both in his mirror, and so to know, adore and love Him".[11]

Here the emphasis is placed on the value of the body and its role within God's plan and its auxiliary function with regard to the soul. In this way, sport itself becomes a precious instrument in promoting "the formation of the complete man and the perfect Christian who thinks and acts according to reason enlightened by the faith".[12]

With an even greater attention and sensibility to the conquests of modern scientific research, John Paul II made the following observation that places the person at the very centre of this activity. He states: "Sport, as you well know, is an activity that involves more than the movement of the body; it demands use of intelligence and the disciplining of the will. It reveals, in other words, the wonderful structure of the human person created by God as a spiritual being, a unity of body and spirit. Athletic activity can help every man and woman to recall that moment when God the Creator gave origin to the human person, the masterpiece of his creative work".[13]

In synthesis, the Magisterium places the human person at the centre of sporting activity, by which his person becomes "perfected" through the simultaneous convergence of all of the human faculties. The person is the irreplaceable, invaluable, and indispensable point of reference for every sporting activity. In this way, sport is directly and synthetically linked to the true identity of the person, as he or she was originally created, and destined for glory.

---

[11] PIUS XII, *Address to Roman Athletes*, May 20, 1945. English translation from R. FEENEY, *op.cit.,* 28. Original Italian text in "Discorsi e radiomessaggi di Pio XII" VII (1945), 56.

[12] PIUS XII, *Address to Cyclists of Giro d'Italia*, June 26, 1946. English translation from R. FEENEY, *op.cit.,* 37. Original Italian text in "Discorsi e radiomessaggi di Pio XII" VIII (1946), 131.

[13] JOHN PAUL II, *Address to participants of Athletic Championship: Be examples of human virtues,* "L'Osservatore Romano" Weekly English Edition, n. 36, September 7, 1987, 5.

Sport in need of "redemption"

Like other human actions, sport can be subject to ambiguous or negative uses that jeopardize its commitment to the integrity of the human person. Pontifical teachings clearly point out the fragility, weakness and ethical contradictions that are present not only in sport itself, but are also found in the person who plays sports and in sporting institutions.

We know well that the person who engages in sport is a sinner like anyone else, and this condition is revealed not only on an individual level but also on a structural level. The task at hand is not a question of simply identifying the "sins" of sport, but of discerning the good wheat from the weeds that are scattered throughout the vast field of sport with all of its complex and multiform activities in the light of an ethic that is rooted in revelation and the fundamental event of salvation.

Because of this, it is quite understandable that the attention of the Church towards the world of sport and athletes has always been characterized by its care to safeguard God's original plan for man which is his sanctification according to the mysterious design of God, manifested in the salvific mission of Jesus Christ.

Sin is present in sport as a sign of fallen human nature. If sport can be seen as a "metaphor of life", it is also accompanied by deviations which appear as cracks in a mirror. These reveal the pressing need for what some have called the "conversion of sport". Sport, which makes up a part of the "all" of that humanity which has been called to salvation in Jesus Christ, is also in need of redemption. Based on the Pauline doctrine of the body, the Pontiffs have often expressed a vigorous appeal for athletes to be aware that they are "temples of the Holy Spirit", and to "glorify God in their bodies" (Cf. *1 Cor* 6: 13-20), exercising a prophetic witness through their good example.

An example of such an appeal was the prayer made by John Paul II at the end of his homily during the Sports Jubilee of 2000, in which the Holy Father prayed with these words: "Jesus, Son of David, have pity on me! "[14] The Pope's example of prayer was a compelling lesson for the vast crowds of sports men and women packed into Rome's Olympic stadium. He then directed everyone's focus to Christ, the "true athlete of God", underlining his intention of proposing Jesus as the effective model for our lives. In the words that followed, the Holy Father referred to Christ as "the more powerful one (cf. *Mk* 1:7), who for our sake confronted and defeated the "opponent", Satan, by the power of the Holy Spirit, thus inaugurating the kingdom of God. He teaches us that to enter into glory we must undergo suffering" (cf. *Lk* 24: 26, 46).[15] By means of the incarnation, sport too is included in the saving work of the redemption, as the very action of a redeemed body.

The Holy Father went on to note that while it is important to identify and promote the many positive aspects of sport, it is only right to also recognize the various transgressions to which it can succumb. He went on to say that "the educational and spiritual potential of sport must make believers and people of good will united and determined in challenging every distorted aspect that can intrude, recognizing it as a phenomenon opposed to the full development of the individual and to his enjoyment of life. Every care must be taken to protect the human body from any attack on its integrity, from any exploitation and from any idolatry. There must be a willingness to ask forgiveness".[16]

The Church clearly recognises the inherent value of sport, but, at the same time, expresses concern for the true authenticity of sport. The Church is attentive to the possible deviations that contradict sport's true purpose and, worse still, that harm the integrity of the person. Because of this, sport is also placed within the realm of human activities that are in need of salvation.

---

[14] JOHN PAUL II, *Homily at the Jubilee for the World of Sport: Even the greatest champions need Christ,* "L'Osservatore Romano" Weekly English Edition, n. 44, November 1, 2000, 1.

[15] *Ibid.*

[16] *Ibid.*

Sport as an ascetic path to human and Christian virtues

Sport's ascetical dimension has always been recognized and the pontiffs have affirmed this often and in numerous ways. As John Paul II noted, "Christian life is like a rather demanding sport, combining all a person's energies to direct them towards the perfection of character, towards a goal which realizes in our humanity 'the measure of Christ's gift' (*Eph* 4:7)".[17] They have exhorted athletes to pursue the sporting ideal, but above all, they have invited them to broaden their perspective of sport so as to include the pursuit of the moral ideals of excellence, and thus reach their integral perfection.[18]

Ancient philosophy taught that "the truth is always in the soul".[19] Accordingly, every human action cannot but manifest the ontological nature of man, since this is the goal towards which all his actions are ultimately directed as a spiritual being. When sport harmoniously enters this process of authentic personal growth, and does so as a practice that is conscious of reaching its goal only through a gradual process of learning that is both interior and exterior, it consequently engages the interior dynamism of "arete" or virtue, as a habit that is practiced in personal and social life.

But, virtue is not reached without acknowledging the soul and without acting accordingly and coherently with this knowledge. Consequently, virtue is the result of an active apprenticeship, just as a skill is acquired in sport. In fact, the relationship between virtue and sport is richly revealed and affirmed in the experience of sport that engages the entire person in all of their faculties and at all levels, whether at the highest level, or the most basic. For it is in playing that we most easily learn how to dominate our passions and orientate them towards a higher goal.

[17] JOHN PAUL II, *Address to conference of Sports and Ethics: Sports can be viewed as a service to mankind*. "L'Osservatore Romano" Weekly English Edition, n. 2, January 8, 1990, 5.

[18] Cf. PAUL VI, *Address to participants of Gira d'Italia*, May 30, 1964, found in G.B. GANDOLFO-L. VASSALLO, *Lo sport nei documenti Pontifici*, La Scuola, Brescia 1994, 151.

[19] PLATO, *The Meno*, 85b.

Because of this, Pius XII taught that the discipline of sport becomes a kind of exercise of human and Christian virtues.[20] In like manner, Paul VI saw sport as a way to teach moral education and asceticism, stating: "There is not a better school for teaching fairness than the exercise of sport for it despises any attempt of cheating as unsportsmanlike. And what asceticism! What an antidote against laziness, indolence and idleness. There is no teacher more demanding than that of sport! How much discipline, how much sacrifice, how much self dominion, courage, and tenacity is required! "[21]

Thus we can say that there can be found in these writings on sporting activity an explicit reference to asceticism and the moral life, in as much as these are present in the intentionality of Christian action. In this way, sport assumes in its historical and anthropological dimension a model of moral action that is especially related to the gratuitous gift of self.

Sport as a valuable educational tool

The Church's teaching regarding sports activity is above all centred in a systematic way on its educational potential and finds in it a means for the integral development of the person. This line of thought is in fact common to all of the papal discourses, whether those that pinpoint sport as a privileged "instrument" for the betterment of the person, or, those that seek to protect the human person from deviations in sport that involve ends that are merely consumerist, materialistic, or even abusive to the body.

The goal then is to awaken by means of a sport that is ever more attentive and responsible, a consciousness of the value of the body in reference to the complete fulfilment of oneself in light of salvation.

---

[20] Cf. Pius XII, *Address to participants of the Italian National Scientific Congress for Sport and Physical Education*, November 8, 1952. English translation from R. Feeney, *op.cit*. 55.

[21] Paul VI, *Address to the International Olympic Committee*, April 22, 1966 [our translation]. Original text found in "Insegnamenti di Paolo VI" IV (1966), 206.

That is, it seeks to take into consideration both the bodily dimension while at the same time being attentive to the promptings of the spirit and above that these are two components that constitute one and the same person.[22] It is precisely because of this, that the Church tends to include sporting activity as in integral part of its pedagogical program.

The primary objective is not simply to foster sports activities for their own sake, but to provide the conditions for building integral characters who can face the drama of life. In fact, when viewed within a moral perspective, life becomes a competition, a fight and a challenge.

In this sense, the teachings of the Magisterium reveal an educative potential of sport that gradually develops in the very practice of this activity. This potential is further verified in their positive behaviour and the fostering of criteria aimed at the development of the subject's personality in accordance with their individual freedom.

Sport in a society of deep-seated changes

The sportsman pope, John Paul II, magnificently elevated sport to a level that was never before considered by the Church. For this much venerated Pontiff, sport had become a "sign of the times". By assigning sport this special category used during the Vatican II Council, he credits sport with a value of important significance in the promotion of the person and opened the door to subsequent reflection in the relationship between sport and spirituality. "In recent years [sport] has continued to grow even more as one of the characteristic phenomena of the modern era, almost a "sign of the times" capable of interpreting humanity's new needs and new expectations".[23] By placing

---

[22] Cf. PIUS XII, *Address to the Italian Sports Centre*, October 9, 1955 in "Discorsi e radiomessaggi di Pio XII" XVII (1955), 279-283.

[23] JOHN PAUL II, *Homily at the Jubilee for the World of Sports: Even the greatest champions need Christ*, October 29, 2000, "L'Osservatore Romano" Weekly English Edition, n. 44, November 1, 2000, 1.

sport in the category of a phenomenon of the modern era, the Pope also recognizes its cultural and civil value.

In this way, sport conveys a meaning that exceeds the mere practice of sport, in as much as it is capable of interpreting life and giving it new meaning in relation to the mystery of the human person. Consequently, the spiritual dimension of sport is fully recovered not as something added on to sport from the outside, but rather, as an intrinsic quality that the sports person manifests in and through the visible gestures of sport.

On the other hand, the global and cultural dimension of sport reveals a new perspective that entails new consequences for human interaction as well as with respect to the many functions inherent to it. Sport, with a language composed of physical gestures that are universally comprehended, crosses over national barriers and constitutes a common denominator that is capable of uniting the entire human community. Because of this, John Paul II urged those involved in this activity "to make sports an opportunity for meeting and dialogue, over and above every barrier of language, race or culture…". He went on to point out that "Sports, in fact, can make an effective contribution to peaceful understanding between peoples and to establishing the new civilization of love".[24]

Such indications on the part of the Magisterium requires us to seek a deeper understanding of the new global dimension of sport and the consequent openness on the part of the Church to these phenomena. This demands careful observation in order to discover the opportunities that present themselves when one contemplates the complex "galaxy" that sport creates. It demands that we look beyond sport itself, to that which it represents symbolically, and to the opportunities that spring up around sport and as a consequence of it.

In this way, the intuition that sport is a cultural phenomenon and an event rich in symbolism and new significance that is valid for the entire world, clearly stands out and calls for a new response. In fact, it

[24] *Ibid.*

calls for a rethinking of a "philosophy" of sport that is adequate for today's multiethnic, multicultural society in the midst of globalization.

Because of this, sport needs a time of conversion. It needs to rediscover itself by means of the exercise of an ongoing spiritual and cultural self-analysis. The essential lines laid out by the pontiffs are directed towards the recovery of a "soul" in sport that can reactivate the mental and spiritual dimensions of the athlete and render sport more capable of realizing its prominent role of transforming society. Here the words of John Paul II assume a prophetic tone as well as mark a path to follow: "Sport, without losing its true nature, can answer the needs of our time: sport that protects the weak and excludes no one, that frees young people from the snares of apathy and indifference, and arouses a healthy sense of competition in them; sport that is a factor of emancipation for poorer countries and helps to eradicate intolerance and build a more fraternal and united world; sport which contributes to the love of life, teaches sacrifice, respect and responsibility, leading to the full development of every human person".[25]

The deeper meaning that emerges from the words of the Pontiff shed light on a double challenge that faces sport. On one hand, there is the task of making use of the universally recognized potential of sport in all its facets to build a more just and fraternal society. On the other hand, lies the task of safeguarding a sport that is rich in human values and determined to reform itself so as to better respond to the integral well being of the person. In a world of profound change, and in need of values and meaning, these are two very concrete tasks that form the basis of a renovated ethical program for the entire sport system. Here, each and every sports person, organism, and institution have their own proper and specific responsibility that they must carry out to the degree in which they bear a social and cultural relevance on sport.

[25] *Ibid.*

The Church "takes the field"

From here we deduce the essential legitimacy of the Church's new task. If the Church seems so interested in sport it is because of the wise and far-sighted discovery of sport as an authentic and appropriate space for special pastoral care and attention.

We can see the Church's desire to dialogue with the world of sport and to encourage this practice. This dialogue has been initiated for good reason. Paul VI perceived the urgency of opening up the doors of the Church to the modern world and saw in sport a field that the Church needs to consciously enter. It does so "with the soul filled with goodness" and because of the mission of "taking all that is beautiful, harmonious, balanced and strong in our human nature and elevating it".[26] He also invited those involved in sport to "discern the criteria for determining its true values and with this same criteria to be committed to engage in dialogue with the world today".[27] In this way, the Church gazes at the complex sporting phenomena, ready and willing to listen to the language of sport and to respond accordingly with a Christian vision that accepts, assumes, perfects and elevates the good in sport, intoning, in this way, an authentic song of life.[28]

Dialogue between the Church and sport produces a specific and competent response on the part of the Church: a "pastoral ministry of sport" that seeks nothing less than a true and proper evangelization. Encouraging us to take action in the field of sport, John Paul II stated: "the Church must be on the front line in order to develop a pastoral ministry that knows how to respond to the needs of sportsmen and to, above all, promote a sport that can create conditions for a life rich in hope".[29]

---

[26] PAUL VI, *Address with occasion of Sports Jubilee Pilgrimage*, November 8, 1975 [our translation]. Original text found in "Insegnamenti di Paolo VI" XIII (1975), 1242.

[27] PAUL VI, *Address to the International Olympic Committee*, April 22, 1966 [our translation]. Original text found in "Insegnamenti di Paolo VI" IV (1966), 208.

[28] See the essay of Cardinal E. PIRONIO, "Sport in the documents of the Pontiffs", in G.B. GANDOLFO-L. VASSALLO (ed.), *Lo sport nei documenti Pontifici*, La Scuola, Brescia 1994, p. 260.

[29] JOHN PAUL II, *Address to Conference of Sports and Ethics: Sports can be viewed as a service to mankind.* "L'Osservatore Romano" Weekly English Edition, n. 2, January 8, 1990, 5.

From here emerges a new approach to sport on the part of the Church. It is not limited to simply encouraging a practice of sport that is in accordance with human and Christian virtues. Rather, this new approach seeks to announce the gospel of salvation from "within" this modern areopagus of sport in order to achieve a motivated and self-conscious "conversion".

Conclusion

Throughout the twentieth century, the consistent teaching of the pontiffs regarding sport has come to form a complex vision that can be synthetically outlined in three phases: the first is the identification of the ethical content in the practice of sport; the second phase, consequently, is that of specifying the inherent and constitutive criteria used in forming and educating the person by means of sporting activity; and lastly, that which directly involves the mission of the Church, the exploration of the multiple ways in which sport can be a vehicle for the proclamation of the gospel.

The Magisterium, while it does not enter into the specific questions of each singular sport's discipline, it nonetheless seeks to point out the opportunities and the potential within sport to contribute to the ongoing project of the integral development of the person, to promote the good example of champions, and to reflect on the role of sport within a society that has ever more global horizons. In conclusion, we can affirm that the "corpus" of papal discourses offers the nucleus for a vision of sport that values sporting activity in all of its complexity and in its totality, whether in the natural order, or in the light of the "history of salvation".

In synthesis, the Church seeks to give proper meaning to the physical dimension of sport, revealing its "humanizing" function. Above all, it seeks to favor sport's potential to elevate the person while at the same time pointing out that it has its limits and must be at the service of God and remain relative to the other higher values and to the superior destiny of the human person.

The goals of the "Church and sport" Section

KEVIN LIXEY, LC*

In light of the analysis of the world of sport from the perspective of history, culture, and the Church's Magisterium, I would now like to briefly review the goals of the "Church and sport" Section. It is our hope that this will serve as an opportunity for an initial discussion and reflection. After going through each one of these goals, I will also propose some concrete plans of action that follow from these aims.

The "Church and sport" Section, officially inaugurated in August 2004, was envisioned with the following aims:

— To insure more direct and systematic attention to the vast world of sport on the part of the Church that fosters a renewal of pastoral work in and through sports.

— To diffuse the teachings of the Church regarding sport and to promote the study and research of various themes of sport, especially those of ethical nature.

— To promote initiatives that can serve to evangelize the world of sport, especially those which foster the witness of an authentic Christian life among professional athletes.

— To promote a culture of sport in harmony with the true dignity of the human person through youth education (schools, oratories, parish centres, lay movements, and other associations).

* Rev. Kevin Lixey, a member of the Congregation of the Legionaries of Christ, is originally from Michigan, USA. He was ordained a priest on January 2, 2001 and since June of 2004, he is the responsible for the new "Church and sport" Section as willed by John Paul II within the Pontifical Council for the Laity.

– *To favour collaboration among the various sporting organizations and associations on the national and international level, serving as a point of reference and dialogue with the various national and international sports entities.*

I. ANALYSIS OF THESE GOALS

To insure more direct and systematic attention to the vast world of sport on the part of the Church that fosters a renewal of pastoral work in and through sports

As we have seen, the Church has directed its attention to the world of sport on various occasions, such as the encounter of Pius XII with Catholic sports associations in 1955; the numerous encounters of professional athletic teams with various pontiffs; and the two Jubilees of Sport held by Pope John Paul II in the Holy Year of 1984 and the Great Jubilee of 2000. To some extent these great events have solicited the need for a section dedicated to sport on the level of the Universal Church. Consequently, its institution by the late Pope John Paul II within the Pontifical Council for the Laity speaks eloquently of the Church's concern for this growing sector of society.

Already in 1945, Pius XII keenly observed: "Both those who accuse the Church of not caring for the body and physical culture, and those who want to restrict her competence and activity to things described as 'purely religious' and 'exclusively spiritual', are far from the truth. It is as if the body, a creation of God like the soul to which it is united, did not have its part to play in the homage to be rendered to the Creator! In the final analysis, what is sport if not a form of education for the body? As it is educational, it is closely related to morality. How then could the Church not care about it?"[1]

---

[1] PIUS XII, *Address to Roman Athletes,* May 20, 1945. English trans. from R. FEENEY, *A Catholic Perspective: Physical Exercise and Sport*, Aquinas Press, Virginia 1995, 28. Original text in "Discorsi e radiomessaggi di Pio XII" VII (1945), 56.

Aware of the important role that sport occupies in the lives of many people, especially the youth, this office, while working directly with the national bishops' conferences and international associations throughout the world, seeks above all to foster a renewal of pastoral ministry within the particular sporting environments at the local level of the Church. After making an initial contact with numerous bishops' conferences and sporting institutions throughout the world, we received several positive responses expressing interest in the creation of this new section and a willingness to collaborate, and many countries had some type of delegate or office dedicated to a pastoral ministry through sport. Furthermore, many inquiries have been made to the Pontifical Council for the Laity in order to know more about this Section and to know what successful pastoral sporting programs already exist or could be implemented.

To diffuse the teachings of the Church regarding sport and to promote the study and research of various themes of sport, especially those of ethical nature.

We were able to discover in this seminar that the pontiffs of the past century have written much more about sport than one may have imagined. Unfortunately, this is not very well known or promulgated. Although there are some selections of the Holy Father's words regarding sporting activity in some languages, there does not exist a "critical edition" of all the writings of the pontiffs on this theme. Certainly, the numerous speeches and writings of the pontiffs do provide a substantial "corpus" for the elaboration of a Christian vision. But, a synthesis of this vision needs to be elaborated and consequently applied to real situations and challenges that face today's parent, coach, trainer, fan, and amateur or professional athlete, as well as the institutions involved in sport.

John Paul II, in an address to participants of a congress on Sport and Ethics, referring especially the aspect of youth formation, observed: "The Church must be in the front ranks in this area, in order to plan a special apostolate adapted to the needs of athletes and especially to promote sports which can create the condition of a life rich in hope".[2] It is important that the "Church and sport" Section respond to the Hoy Father's appeal. In addition to promoting a Christian vision of sport, this section will serve to coordinate studies on the various ethical questions and problems that specifically involve the world of sport.

To promote initiatives that can serve to evangelize the world of sport, especially those which foster the witness of an authentic Christian life among professional athletes.

Numerous groups of professional athletes have been received by the pontiffs of the last century. Aware of the great relevance sport has in the lives of youth, as well as the important responsibility professional athletes have as role models for the multitudes of young people who look up to them, the Church has consistently encouraged them to live up to this responsibility. John Paul II, had this to say to professional players: "The eyes of sport fans throughout the world are fixed on you. Be conscious of your responsibility! It is not only the champion in the stadium but also the whole person who should become a model for millions of young people, who need 'leaders', not 'idols'. They need men who can convey to them the zest for challenge, a sense of discipline, the courage to be honest and the joy of unselfishness".[3]

The Church cannot be absent from this important sphere. In fact, we have heard from the testimony of athletes during the course of this seminar that the world of professional sport needs the Church much more than the Church needs the world of sport! How can the

---

[2] JOHN PAUL II, *Address to conference of Sports and Ethics: Sports can be viewed as a service to mankind,* "L'Osservatore Romano" Weekly English Edition, n. 2, January 8, 1990, 5.

[3] JOHN PAUL II, *Blessing of Rome's Olympic Stadium: Pope inaugurates 'Italia 90' Cup,* "L'Osservatore Romano" Weekly English Edition, n. 24, June 11, 1990, 3-4.

"Church and sport" Section support those efforts that reach out to professional athletes? Naturally, a pastoral ministry to professional athletes can most effectively be carried out on the national and local level where the players spend most of their time. Whereas the task of this Section is that of assisting in the coordination of activities and events on the international level. In order to reach these objectives, perhaps another event on the level of the Jubilee of Sports could be organized, or perhaps an international association of professional Catholic athletes or other initiatives that encourage champions in the living of their faith could also be promoted.

To promote a culture of sport in harmony with the true dignity of the human person through education (schools, oratories, parish centres, lay movements, and other associations).

Various Pontiffs have pointed out the formative role that sport can play in education. As Pius XII eloquently noted: "Sport, properly directed, develops character, makes a person courageous, a generous loser, and a gracious victor; it refines the senses, gives intellectual penetration, and steels the will to endurance. Sport is an occupation of the whole person, and while perfecting the body as an instrument of the mind, it also makes the mind itself a more refined instrument for the search and communication of truth".[4]

Catholic schools, oratories and clubs at the parish level, and Catholic sports associations and youth movements offer an extensive and valid network through which the formative aspects of sport can be promoted in order to serve the integral formation of the person. But, it is necessary to ensure that sports programs and sporting activities actually are directed towards this end of youth formation. Because of this, special concern should be given to those who work with youth in order that be made aware of the transcendence of their important formative role.

---

[4] Pius XII, *Message to the Central Sports School of the Armed Forces,* July 29, 1945, "Discorsi e Radiomessaggi del Pio XII", vol. VII, 129.

Given the strong educational component in athletic disciplines, this Section will seek to favour the affirmation of a sporting culture that is at the service of the human person by promoting concrete formation programs for youth. In light of this, we can recall how much the World Youth Days have done to renew youth ministry! Today, youth ministry, in great part, enjoys a dynamic dimension that it did not have before. The important catechetical dimension is now complemented by an experience of the faith. Perhaps a similar application could be made to the world of youth sports so that sporting activities also become a place for a "socialization of the faith"[5] – that is, a place where the faith is lived and experienced as well as taught.

Pope John Paul II in an address to the Italian Sports Centre (which works primarily with Catholic sports clubs and parish oratories throughout Italy), encouraged the directors and staff with these words that we can apply to all educators: "My venerated Predecessor, the servant of God Pius XII, then asked your Sodality to be the leaven of Christianity in stadiums, on roads, on mountains, at sea, wherever your banner is raised with honour. In the course of the years, dear friends, you have tried to stay faithful to this behest, presenting the Italian Sports Centre as a school for authentic human formation. You have toiled to acquaint children, young people and adults with the riches and beauty of the Gospel, through various types of sports. You have helped them to encounter Jesus and choose him as their ultimate raison d'être. Still today this is your mission, and society still needs it. The efforts of your association to promote sport as a formative experience in the parishes, schools and throughout the territory, will help the young generations to choose and to foster the authentic values of life".[6]

---

[5] Cf. BENEDICT XVI, *Meeting with diocesan clergy of Aosta: What the 'Grain of Wheat' teaches us today,* "L'Osservatore Romano" Weekly English Edition, n. 31, August 3, 2005, 4.

[6] JOHN PAUL II, *Address to the Italian Sports Centre: Called to be Christ's witnesses in sport,* June 26, 2004, "L'Osservatore Romano" English Edition, n. 28, July 14, 2004, 3.

To favour collaboration among the various sporting organizations and associations on the national and international level, serving as a point of reference and dialogue with the various national and international sports entities.

The role that sports organizations and associations play must not be overlooked. The associations and institutions set policies and procedures that can either succeed or fail in enabling sport to be a significant vehicle for the promotion of human values. Without these values, as John Paul II pointed out, sport would be reduced to mere effort and to a questionable, soulless demonstration of pure physical strength.[7] I would like to recall his address to the Union of European Football Associations, in which he called for a collaborative effort among sports entities in order to ensure that sport does not lose its formative potential: "In contemporary society football is a widespread sporting activity which involves a great number of people. [...] This fact emphasizes the responsibility of those who look after the organization and promote the spread of this sporting activity at the professional and amateur level. They are called never to lose sight of the significant educational possibilities which football, like other similar sporting disciplines, can develop. Furthermore, given the spread of this sport, it would be good if promoters, organizers at different levels and communications personnel engaged in concerted efforts to ensure that football never loses its genuine characteristic of being a sporting activity, and that it is not submerged by other concerns, especially economic ones".[8]

These words of John Paul II have much to say to all sports institutions. By following these indications, Catholic sports organizations can

---

[7] Cf. JOHN PAUL II, *Address to participants of the Giro d'Italia: An important vehicle of lofty human values*, "L'Osservatore Romano" Weekly English Edition, n. 21, May 24, 2000, 8.

[8] JOHN PAUL II, *Address to members of the UEFA: You are models for young people*, "L'Osservatore Romano" Weekly English Edition, n. 20, May 17, 2000, 6.

join forces in order to work towards this same goal: a sport at the service of the human person, and not the person at the service of sport. I believe this objective is already being realized by means of this international seminar in which we have been exchanging ideas and learning from the experiences of others.

II. Some concrete plans of action

Construct a sports network

As we have seen in the course of these days, the world of sport is as vast as it is complex. Because of this, it is crucial for this Section to establish contact with the various sport institutions and build a network of persons (university professors, sport association directors, representatives from national bishop conferences, sports professionals, etc.) with diverse expertise in order to have the resources and means to help us achieve our objectives. Thus, our immediate priority is that of expanding our network among the bishop conferences, as well as with the various Catholic sports associations. "Church and sport" will also continue to make contact with the major international sports institutions.

Elaboration of a Christian vision of sport

Although it is not proper to speak of a "Christian" sport, it is fitting to speak of how Christianity specifically enlightens sporting activity by offering a discernment criteria and by broadening its horizons. From its beginning, "Church and sport" has been gathering and studying the teachings of the Magisterium of the Church regarding sport, in order to compile an adequate bibliography for the elaboration of a Christian vision of sport. For this end, it will be necessary on one hand to continue an ongoing study of the teachings of the pontiffs, while on the other hand, remaining in continual contact with the world of sport to know up close its needs and to delineate the fundamental points of a vision of sport that can adequately respond to the particular problems and challenges within the world of sport today.

Develop some suggested guidelines for a pastoral ministry to sport

In order to be of real assistance to the bishop's conferences and sports associations, the Section will continue to gather information from youth sports ministry from around the world about the "best practices", that is, some of the most effective ways sport is being incorporated into youth ministry on various levels. We are also exploring the best way to make all of this information available to all. In this perspective and for this purpose, it would be convenient to hold a future encounter with those who work in the pastoral ministry of sport within the national bishop conferences and within international sporting associations in order to provide a further analysis of these pastoral sports programs that are already in place.

A look at our future commitment

JOSEF CLEMENS*

We have spent the last two days examining sport from different points of view: sport as a social phenomenon, as a leisure activity, as an educational tool for young people, and as a means of evangelisation. While looking at the positive aspects, we have also identified some of its contradictions. Pius XII once noted that physical competition has the potential to become a means of fostering human and Christian values. "That is –he said- indeed what it ought to become, and be, so that the practice of sport can surpass itself...and be preserved from materialistic deviations which would impair its value and lower its nobility".[1] Now, where do we want to go? What specific direction do we wish to take? What are our priorities? It would appear that the first natural step which the "Church and sport" section should take is to become a significant point of reference for the world of sport, both inside and outside the Church. A point of reference for what? To communicate a Christian vision of sport, in its educational, pastoral and social dimensions. It is a task that requires both the skill to elaborate this vision and the ability to communicate it effectively.

I. BUILDING ON PAST TRADITIONS

As we have seen, the Church has her own vision of sport that has developed across the years ever since the Pontificate of Pius XII. Even

---

* Mgr Josef Clemens was ordained a priest for the German diocese of Paderborn in 1976. From 1984 to 2003 he was the personal secretary of the then Cardinal Ratzinger. At the end of 2003, he was appointed Secretary of the Pontifical Council for the Laity, and was ordained bishop on January 6, 2004.

[1] PIUS XII, *Address to the National Scientific Congress on Sport*, November 8, 1952 [our translation]. Original text found in "Discorsi e radiomessaggi" XIV (1952), 389.

though the Magisterium of the Church has written a great deal about sport, most Catholics – and particularly those who are directly engaged in sport – are unaware of the Church's teaching. This vision could certainly be further developed, and there is no doubt that it should continually be re-proposed, and effectively communicated to the entire sports world. On the back of the seminar's programme you will have noticed the photograph of a basketball game being played in St. Peter's Square in the presence of Pius XII. How did this come about? In 1955, Pope Pius XII had convened a meeting in Rome with all the Catholic National Sports Federations to celebrate the 10th anniversary of the Italian Sports Centre. Years later, John Paul II celebrated a Jubilee of Sports in Rome's Olympic Stadium in the Holy Year of the Redemption in 1983-84 and during the Great Jubilee of 2000.

In addition, the pontiffs have frequently met with delegations of athletes and professional sports teams during the past twenty-five years. These events have had a major impact and have penetrated into the professional sporting environment, particularly in Europe, even though they may not have had the same resonance in other continents. They have provided a major opportunity for the pontiffs to communicate the message of the Church to the sports world. It therefore seems obvious that one of the essential tasks of this new Section is to continue building on this tradition.

II. POINT OF REFERENCE WITHIN THE CHURCH

At the present time only about a dozen of the two hundred some Bishops' Conferences in the world have an office dedicated to relations between the Church and sport. I am convinced that the more familiar the Bishops' Conferences become with this section and its purposes, the greater interest they will show in establishing an office or nominating a reference person for the pastoral service to sport. This interest will grow as the Section becomes more relevant, and as an effective pastoral ministry is developed to better attend to the world of sport.

In addition to the Catholic international sports associations, which are particularly numerous in Europe, the new phenomenon of the Ecclesial Movements and the New Communities has given rise to other types of Catholic sports associations which are somewhat similar to the European associations of FICEP and FISEC which have existed for many years. Similarly, these new associations pursue internationally objectives and concern more than one of the various Bishops' Conferences. This is why they would be best placed in a kind of wider federation or "forum" of Catholic international sports associations, linked to the Pontifical Council for the Laity which would provide them with advice and assistance in their common mission of promoting sport as a frontier of the new evangelization. In fact, the directors and personnel of these associations need to be assisted in order that they can promote Christian values and the faith itself and thus become a leaven within the world of sport. Otherwise, how can we expect secular sports associations to promote human values if these Catholic associations are not committed to promoting Christian values?

In the course of the discussions at our seminar mention has been made of the need to encourage Catholic athletes to be responsible role models for the numerous young people who look up to them. We see some promising initiatives being made in various countries. However, given the national and international scope of these efforts, sustaining spiritual attention to these athletes becomes an international challenge. In this regard, it would be good to examine the possible ways that the Church, and this Section in particular, can assist Catholic athletes in giving witness to their faith and explore ways in which they can cooperate in various youth ministry events at the national or the international levels.

Finally, the world of sport has need of an authoritative voice from the part of the Church. We have seen how far money and ambition can drive athletes and coaches, and even parents, to push athletes beyond their natural limits and often to the detriment of their health.

The Church has always defended the human person from threats imposed by secular society, and she must also uphold the dignity of the person from a sporting environment that seeks to use people as means to an end such as for economic gain or for fame. From the reaction of the international sports world to the institution of this new Section, we have seen the great interest in, and the great expectations aroused by this new initiative of the Catholic Church, and in particular the Holy See, in international governmental and non-governmental organisations. Because the positions adopted by the Church are contributions of a "non-partisan" institution, with no nationalistic or financial interests, this enhances the Church's effectiveness and credibility in the world of sport. As an "expert in humanity" the Church's position on fundamental and ethical issues is acceptable if not to all, at least to very many people.

III. Towards the New Evangelisation

As we have seen, the idea of sport as "a playing field rich in opportunities" is directly related to the call to the new evangelisation, the Christian mission to proclaim the Gospel to the modern world. One of John Paul II's favourite themes has certainly been taken up by Pope Benedict XVI. In his address to the German bishops in Cologne on World Youth Day, the Holy Father appealed to them in the following words: "Dear Brothers, as you yourselves said in your Pastoral Letter of September 21, 2004, on the occasion of the Jubilee of St. Boniface: 'We have become a mission land'. This is true for large parts of Germany. I therefore believe that throughout Europe, and likewise elsewhere, we should give serious thought as to how to achieve a true evangelisation in this day and age; not only a new evangelisation, but often a true and proper first evangelisation. People do not know God, they do not know Christ. There is a new form of paganism and it is not enough for us to strive to preserve the existing flock, although this is very important: we must ask the important question: what really is life? I believe we must all try together to find new ways of bringing the Gospel to the contemporary world, of proclaiming Christ anew and of implanting the faith".[2]

Let me end with a few general remarks. The exceptional events that have occurred this year – the death of Pope John Paul II, the election of Pope Benedict XVI and the World Youth Day in Cologne – have had worldwide resonance, perhaps unprecedented in history, even among many sports men and women, managers and trainers and sports associations. Today, we can humbly recognize a new receptiveness to questions of faith, and also to their ethical consequences. It is no coincidence that many famous sports men and women have asked to be received or greeted by the new Pope over this period. Let us take advantage of this "*kairos*" also for our new "Church and sport" Section. A joint debate on such pressing issues in sport as doping, for example, could lead to a deeper reflection on the fundamental elements of Christian anthropology which certainly has something to say in this field. The new section could therefore become a "bridge" within the world of sport between believers and non believers, and between Christians and people of other faiths.

I urge you very carefully to consider the field of opportunity that lies before each one of you, some of you in the academic world, others in the pastoral ministry to young people, and others still in the world of professional sport. We place our trust in your generous co-operation and your future help. The effectiveness of the "Church and sport" Section depends on your response and the effectiveness of your actions in your particular field. Thanking you once again for your generous participation, I invite you: "*Duc in altum*", to pull out into the deep and to cast your nets into the sea.

---

[2] BENEDICT XVI, *Address to German Bishops in Cologne: A symphony of faith,* "L'Osservatore Romano" Weekly English Edition, n. 38, August 31, 2005, 3.

I. ROUND TABLE

Problems and challenges in sports today

INTRODUCTION

VINCENT CAPUANO, S.I.*

It seems to me that all the diverse themes of this seminar can be divided into three groups: Philosophic and theological considerations of the theory of sport, practical and pastoral considerations of sport as a tool for the new evangelization, and considerations of ethical problems in sport. This round table discussion will consider this ethical dimension. What is the objective of this academic exercise called a roundtable conversation and what is the objective of my introductory comments? This round table proposes to examine four different relationships: sport related to business, sport related to violence, sport related to doping, and sport related to the media. Each panellist will examine the problems and challenges that exist in a particular relationship.

During seminary studies the rule was oft repeated: "Never affirm, seldom deny, always distinguish. What I intend to do in these introductory comments is to make some distinctions that may help clarify what will be discussed. I want to say three things: 1) How I think sport is distinguished from other activities, 2) How I think we can distinguish various ways of experiencing and talking about sport and 3) How I see our task as Christian thinkers is distinguished from that of secular thinkers.

How do we distinguish sport from other human activity? Before

---

* Rev. Vincent Capuano was born in 1954. Before entering the Congregation of the Jesuits in the Province of Maryland, he coached basketball at Theil University in Pennsylvania. As a Jesuit, he has worked at the University of Gonzaga in Spokane, where, besides being an assistant basketball coach, he began working on a doctorate about the relationship between sport and virtue. Presently, he teaches theology and philosophy in Salta, Argentina, as well as the regional coordinator of the "Fe y Alegría" Schools.

we can talk about problems in sport we should have some idea of what sport is. Is sport fundamentally play? Or is it basically competition? Or is it playful competition or is it competitive play? Or are some sports play and others competition? It is clear from the start that these two categories "play" and "competition", need to be dealt with. I suggest that sport is competitive play. That is to say that sport is a subspecies of play and not of competition.

How can we distinguish different levels of discourse used when talking about sport or different ways of experiencing sport? One of the problems when reading articles about problems in sport is the confusion in regards to what John Loy called level of discourse. John Loy identified multiple uses of the term sport and described different levels of discourses each of which treats sport in a different manner.[1] I think that there are not only different levels of discourse but there are also different ways of experiencing competitive play i.e., sport. There are four categories of sport experience: 1) As a basic play experience; 2) as a practice; 3) as an institutionalized game; 4) as a social phenomenon.

Sport as a basic play experience is play for play's sake. It is the experience of child's play, pickup games, game occurrences and spontaneous play. It is the experience of players and games.

The second way we experience sport is as a practice. Here I borrow the term practice from Alasdair MacIntyre.[2] A practice involves a replication of basic play experiences or game occurrences. Practices are what players do in order to play games. Practices involve habits and culture. Practices are concerned with internal goods, they include activities that help its practitioners play games. Thus basketball players

---

[1] J. LOY, *The Nature of Sport: A definitional effort*, in "Quest" vol. X, May 1968, 1-15.

[2] See A. MACINTIRE, *After Virtue*, (2nd Ed.) Notre Dame, Indiana 1984, 187, where practice is defined as "a coherent and complex form of socially established cooperative human activity through which goods internal to that form of activity are realized in the course of trying to achieve those standards of excellence which are appropriate to, and partially definitive of, that form of activity, with the result that human powers to achieve excellence, and human conceptions of ends and goods involved are systematically extended".

will shoot layups, do defensive drills and listen to chalk talks, all of which are not strictly speaking playing basketball but help attain goods internal to the practice of basketball. They develop habits that make playing more enjoyable and easier.

The third way to experience sport is as institutionalized play. As such it is concerned not only with internal goods but external ones as well. Such institutions serve to assure that game occurrences are repeated and supposed to work for "the good of the game". Baseball is a practice, baseball clubs and leagues are institutions.

The fourth way to experience sport is as a social phenomenon. Here one includes social institutions, orders, contexts and situations. Sport as a social phenomenon includes many activities that are related to basic game experiences and practices but are only marginally concerned with internal goods of a game. Here we include sporting goods manufacturers, sports broadcasters, sports bars, gamblers, etc.

Keeping these four ways of experiencing sport clear in our mind will help when we set ourselves to the tasks of analyzing the problems and challenges in sport. For example when examining the relationship between sport and business we would need to distinguish the relation between the basic root experience of play and business, from the relation between the practice of a sport and business, from the relation between institutionalized games and business, from the relation between the social phenomenon of sport and business.

Lastly, I think we should distinguish our task as Christian thinkers from that of secular thinkers. Perhaps as we listen to the presentations we could begin to think about how we as Christians could contribute to the analysis of the problems precisely as Christian thinkers. How can the dogmas of our Faith help us to find solutions that non-believers will have more trouble discovering? How does our personal relation with Jesus Christ change how we view other relations: the relation between sport and business, the relation between sport and violence, the relation between sport and doping, and the relation between sport and media?

Sport and business

CLARK POWER*

I approach the topic of business and sport as an "outsider" in that I am neither a scholar of business nor a business person. On the other hand, I accepted the invitation to address this topic because of my experiences as a developmental psychologist studying sports and character development, as a former youth sports coach, and as a member of a university with a legendary football program.

Nothing has changed sports as much over the last thirty years for good or for ill than what is commonly referred to as the "commercialization of sport". I do not mean that the commercialization of sport is something new or that commercialization has only recently had an influence on the way we play and watch sports. Rather, I want to call attention to the way in which commercialization is transforming our playing and watching, and even more significantly the way in which sport is being used to transform basic human values.

Before I begin to sketch a portrait of the business side of sports, I would like to offer a few brief comments about the value of sports themselves and the challenges that commercialization poses. I believe Michael Novak makes a convincing case that we can only account for the attraction of sports for both the participant and spectator by acknowledging that sports originate in a deeply religious spirit. Sports evoke remarkable commitment and make possible stunning human

* Prof Clark Power received a doctorate in the educational sciences from the University of Harvard, and presently teaches at the University of Notre Dame. He is currently working in partnership with the Center for Sport, Spirituality and Character Development at Neumann College in Philadelphia and other programs that promote the role of a coach as a youth minister. Among other works, he is the author of *Character Psychology and Education* and *The challenge of Pluralism; Education, Politics and Values*.

achievements. Inherently religious, sports are also play. As Novak (1994) puts it, "Play belongs to the Kingdom of Ends; work to the Kingdom of Means. Barbarians play in order to work; the civilized work in order to play".[1] Finally sports at their best can serve as an "instrument for the moral and spiritual elevation of the human person"[2] to quote John Paul II. In fact, both he and now Pope Benedict XVI have emphasized the particular character building dimension of youth sports. In describing the commercialization of sports, I will pay particular attention to the context of youth sports, particularly in North America.

PRIZES AND REWARDS

Payoffs for winning at different levels of sport are increasing. The media play a major role in this. Note for example increased television coverage of "tournament" play. As rewards increase, the pressure to win increases and inequalities between winners and losers grow. Rewards discriminate against the poor: rising to the elite levels of sports is influenced by income, education, social status.

Prizes and rewards have their value. Crowns, cups, laurel wreathes express the importance attached to the contest, recognize and celebrate the achievement. Prize money provides compensation for athletes allowing them more time to train and to perfect their skills. Prize money also lures the very best to compete against each other.

Excessive rewards can, however, tip the proper balance between winning and competing. Extrinsic rewards can undermine intrinsic motivation. The temptation to cheat, risk injury, or use performance enhancing substances grows as ends seem to justify means (win at any cost mentality). Rewards also focus on elite athletes and teams at the expense of others, which reduces the competitive pool.

---

[1] M. NOVAK, *The Joy of Sport,* Madison Books, Maryland 1967, xvii.
[2] JOHN PAUL II, *Address to the National Italian Olympic Committee* [our translation]. Italian text can be found in "Insegnamenti di Giovanni Paolo II" II,2 (1979), 1471.

Rewards can also turn sports increasingly into an instrument for personal advancement. In the United States, many parents and their children view youth sports as an avenue to a college scholarship and to a lucrative sports career. Additionally, the benefits of sports success seem to lead many parents and their children to see sports as means of escaping from poverty. Although the odds of making a high paying professional team are only about 1 in 12,000, parents and their children at all educational levels persist in believing that their child is one of the chosen few.

Although the rewards of sports appear to be "earned" through commitment and hard work, those at the elite levels of sports tend to be privileged by income, education, social status.[3] The costs of participating in sports at the elite levels is rapidly increasing partly as a result of advancements in sport physiology and the technology of training and partly as a result of a crazed ambition to seek out the best coaches, trainers, and competition. In my neighbourhood, parents will spend thousands of dollars each year to provide their twelve-year old superstar with a personal trainer, sports summer camps, and membership on an elite "travel team".

Finally as Coakley and other sport sociologists have noted,[4] the increased rewards that accrue to the "winners" reinforce a "success ideology". Sports legitimize the capitalist work ethic by propagating the view that hard work leads to success and to entitlement to the rewards of success. Sports heroes become moral exemplars on the basis of one virtue – hard work. In fact, taken in isolation from other virtues, hard work itself may become an obsession carried at the expense of other virtues, such as justice and prudence.

BUSINESS AS SUBSIDIZER AND SPONSOR: ACCESS, AVAILABILITY, AND VARIETY

We need money to pay for sports equipment and playing areas, we need money to make greater sports participation possible for those

---

[3] Cf. J. COAKLEY, *Inside Sports: Using Sociology to Understand Athletes and Sport Experiences,* Taylor & Francis, 1999.
[4] *Ibid.*

who may otherwise be unable to play for reasons of poverty or physical and mental handicaps (e.g., Special Olympics). Money has also led to the proliferation of non-traditional sports (e.g. skating and snowboarding), to increased opportunities to follow various teams through increased media coverage. Unfortunately the money available for sports is unevenly distributed, the poor lack opportunities provided to the rich, elite sports programmes may be well-funded but little financial support is given to other programs.

Sponsorship is becoming the primary means of supporting sports and sponsorship creates identifications with and obligations to the sponsor (e.g., Nike pays colleges for exclusive rights for sports apparel). Public-spirited donors are being replaced by private entrepreneurs who see their sponsorship as an investment and expect a return. In the United States, we are witnessing a disturbing pattern of tax money being raised to fund stadiums for the use of privately owned teams. With limited ticket availability and rising costs, few of the fans who pay for these stadiums can actually attend the games.

The Business of Sports

Sports are one of the fastest-growing industries in the United States and throughout the world. The sports industry is currently valued at 213 billion dollars, just below banking at 266 billion dollars and transportation at 256 billion dollars. Sports like tennis, soccer, and golf are becoming increasingly global and national sports leagues, such as the United States' NBA (National Basketball Association) are reaching out to expanding global markets (e.g., NBA promoted its Olympic "Dream Team," which then created market for NBA in over 100 countries). Sports are also becoming a marketing tool for all kinds of products sold throughout the world (e.g., Nike, Adidas, Gatorade, Cheerios, Coca Cola, Budweiser). Much of the financial success of sports is due to the influence of the media. Television contracts for sports are skyrocketing. In 1964, NBC paid $600,000 for the right to telecast the Olympics. Today, NBC is paying 2.3 billion dollars for the rights to televise the Olympics in Athens, Turin, and Beijing.

The commercialization of sports makes more money available to subsidize sports. Moreover, media coverage makes greater involvement with teams and athletes possible. On the other hand, the commercialization of sports increases inequalities and "feeds" the materialistic culture it depends upon. Commercialized sports thrive under certain conditions: market economies, urban areas, significant proportion of population wealthy enough to pay for the "luxury" of attendance at sport events or participation in sport clubs, and a materialistic culture in which possessing sports merchandise and associating oneself with a sports team becomes important to one's sense of self-worth. As sports become commercialized, athletes become "commodities" for the market. Many fear not only what this does to the athletes but to those who identify with them.

In the interest of attracting every larger audiences, sports become spectacle, sometimes at great human cost. Television focuses on thrills, daring, and violence. Witness the rising in popularity of the of the X-games (featuring risky moves and high tech equipment) and "professional" wrestling. Is it a surprise or a concern to learn that young American males rate wrestling as their second favourite spectator sport behind American football? The deeper values and aesthetics of sports get lost when sports become produced for mass audiences who lack the expertise needed to appreciate the beauty of finer points of the play of the game. Sports events are now much more than the athletic contest itself – note half-time shows, cheerleaders, television screens built into scoreboards advertising at every break in the action. We should also take note that gambling on sports in the United States is a $50 billion business and rapidly growing thanks to the internet.

In the area of youth sports, children are becoming viewed by their parents and corporate sponsors as "an investment" and children are targeted as consumers of sports products (e.g., soccer and basketball shoes) and services (special sports camps). Sports businesses invest in youth sport programs to cultivate future markets (30 million children in youth sports in North America under direction of 4.5 million coaches and 1.5 million administrators). Note, however, there is little funding for education that prepares coaches to meet the developmental needs of children.

Where do we go from here? Today's commercialized world of sports challenges us to rediscover sports' basic meaning and value. If sports express our religious longings, free us in play, and offer us means of spiritual and moral elevation, then we must find effective ways meeting the challenges that business poses to sport today.

Sport and violence

ELAINE RAAKMAN*

Violence in sport is most often envisioned in terms of fan violence: massive stadiums filled with unruly spectators such as the infamous hooligans. This group behavioural disorder continues to be a problem today and is emblematic of greater societal problems. In fact, as fan violence has become an increasingly popular theme of study, sociologists and academics point to such factors as unemployment, the disenfranchisement of youth, and the regional clustering of individuals belonging to a particular class as contributing directly to this unruly behaviour.[1] Certainly, confronting the issue of violence in professional sporting events is an important task, since there is a fear that children will emulate the behaviour they witness when watching professional sporting events. It is also a task made more difficult by the fact that the world of sport has become an enormous financial enterprise that is generally administered by faceless corporations.

Yet, while the formative or de-formative role of the professional sporting environment should certainly not be underestimated, what I would like to focus on today is something closer to home, namely, violence in youth sport. Research shows that the experience of children in their own sporting environment is at least as important, if not more important in teaching what constitutes acceptable and unacceptable

* Elaine Raakman is from Canada. While obtaining her degree in sports management from Brock University in Canada, she developed a program that offers educational institutions the means by which they can regulate and identify problematic behaviour in juvenile sports. This led her to found the non-for-profit, "Just Play Sport Services" (cf. www.wejustplay.com) which today is tool that assists public and private schools in the Australia, Canada, and the U.S. to avoid violence and misbehaviour in youth sports.

[1] See the article of G. PILZ, *Social Factors Influencing Sport and Violence* in "Concilium", September 1989, 32-43.

conduct, than that of the professional sporting environment. Further-more, research also shows that youth coaches are extremely important role models in demonstrating what is to be expected from those par-ticipating in sports. Lastly, the field of youth sports is also the place where the most effective changes for the better can be made as they form the foundation upon which all other sport behaviour is built. As cyclist Lance Armstrong once said: "A team is just another version of a community. The same principles apply to any communal undertak-ing, whether you're talking about a community garden, a neighbour-hood watch, or a race around France: if you want something, first you have to give it. You have to invest in it".[2] Likewise, if we want youth sports to be rid of violence, we have to invest in this; we have to ensure that youth sports programs and structures are truly formative and not de-formative.

It is unfortunate to learn that unacceptable behaviour has become rampant in today's youth sports. These problems range from the ubiq-uitous verbal abuse and harassment to the more severe, yet increas-ingly frequent, forms of physical abuse. Some recent examples of deviant behaviour in youth sports in the past few years include: coaches instructing players to physically injure opponents; verbal and physical assault of officials by players, coaches and spectators; parents, including mothers, exposing themselves to other parents or children; a father of a player choking his son's coach to unconsciousness; the list goes on and in some incidences has resulted in death such as the Junta-Costin incident in Boston in 2003.

Worse still is that this violence is occurring in an environment that is "supposed to be" educational, as people still consider sport to be beneficial for children to learn physical, mental and behavioural skills that will help them mature as persons. In fact, many youth sports pro-grams were originally envisioned as a healthy means of recreation where children could develop such social skills as friendship and citi-zenship. The potential for sport to foster these benefits is enormous,

[2] L. ARMSTRONG - S. JENKINS, *Every Second Counts*, Broadway 2004, 166.

yet the potential for harm is equally great. In recent years we have come to understand that sport does not inherently build character. Some argue that it only reveals character.[3] In order for sport to build character, sport programs must be structured and monitored in such a way to support and encourage the values and principles that foster character building.

Sports psychologists and researchers attribute "unsportsmanlike" conduct that permeates youth sports to such factors as the ever increasing emphasis on winning, over invested parental interest, insufficiently trained coaches, exacerbated professionalism, the negative demeanour of top athletes, and the erosion of social values. Regardless of the reasons, the ultimate outcome of negative sport environment may have long-term effects that can be far more serious than the present behaviour problems at sporting events themselves. Studies reveal that participants in sports environments that permit or support negative conduct (either deliberately or inherently) are more likely to display, adopt and justify antisocial comportment outside the sport environment.

Beyond mere good will, there is a real need of accountability and measurement in sports programs in order to effectively indicate whether programs implemented to improve or reduce the frequency of misconduct are indeed effective. While sport agencies around the world were directing considerable resources towards managing these problems, no formalized feedback systems were being implemented to objectively assess the effectiveness of their interventions. This motivated me to start *Justplay Sport Services,* as a means to help sports administrators identify the sources and conditions that contribute directly to problem behaviour in order to effectively correct them. It also helps administrators to identify and understand the comportment

---

[3] Cf. L. HOWE, *Athletics, Embodiment, and the Appropriation of the Self* in "The Journal of Speculative Philosophy" – Vol. 17, Number 2, Penn State Univ. Press 2003, 92-107; or D. CARR, *What moral education significance has physical education?* in M.J. MCNAMEE – S.J. PARRY "Ethics and Sport", Spon Press 1998, 119-131.

trends (both positive and negative) within a given sport environment so that it is possible to create and maintain policies and standards that ensure that sport is affecting our youth, families and communities in a positive manner.

After five years of monitoring various sports at the community, provincial (state) and national level, we have noted some important trends. The discussion of these trends is beyond the scope of this presentation. However, some of the more disconcerting trends we have identified are the following:[4] *a)* Problem behaviour occurs in all sports we monitor, from 20% to 37% of the time (This is far more than 'a few bad apples'!); *b)* In all sports, coaches were the number one cause of misbehaviour from 30% to sometimes 50% of the time. Players are second at approximately 27%, and spectators are third, at a mere 18%; *c)* Officials also indicated that poor coach and player behaviour more adversely affects officials than poor spectator behaviour; *d)* Upwards of 70% of all misconduct occurs during regular season games, in home league divisions, as opposed to play-off games or more elite skill levels.

In conclusion, we can see that behaviour begins at home – at the weekly practice or game- and much depends on the coach or parent! If he or she is a "good sport", so goes the rest of the team. If, on the other hand, there is only concerned about their own ego, this will also be reflected in the team. Peace has a price. If we want to rid sport of violence, something has to go. I suggest that the individual "ego" of the coach, spectator-parent, or player be sacrificed for the good of the team. In fact, the etymology of the word 'community' is "friendship based on shared interests" and that of the word 'team' means "being yoked together". A team is another form of community. All of us have the opportunity to build a team at the community level. I invite all of us to allow our shared interest in sport to yoke us together in this common endeavour to rid sport of violence for the good of our youth.

---

[4] See the website: http://www.wejustplay.com/workshops/coaching_for_character/pdf.dataresults

Sport and media

The relationship between sport and the media today is "particularly risky" and prone to conflict. It is marked by a strong sense of malaise which almost always breaks out into a kind of "war" between the sports industry and the news industry, both of which are firmly set on defending their own, putative, autonomy.

The reason for this conflict between sport and the media is that the sports world has its own structures, rules, powers, controlling bodies and its own courts, and very often the news media demand entry into that world, to become familiar with it and to talk about it. What is missing is a healthy relationship of cooperation between them, beyond the traditional technical information that sport needs, and which the media duly supply.

I am not trying to hide behind a corporatist attitude. For quite some time I have taken a critical stance, recognizing "our" and "my" faults which include reporting only about the wrongdoings in the world of sport, ignoring the good things that are being done, and the positive stories and examples which sport knows how to offer and continues to do so. These positive things are certainly less newsworthy, and the public is less interested in them because it is always far too keen on scandals and gossip, exclusively attracted by pushing the process of spectacularization to the extreme.

* Fabrizio Maffei, journalist and television host, was born in Rome in 1955, and has become one of the most familiar faces on the RAI Sport TV channel, which he has headed for the past two years. After graduating in law he chose journalism in preference to the legal profession. He has been the host of such programmes as *Domenica sportiva* and *90th Minute*, and has been a broadcaster at the Olympics in Moscow, Barcelona and Los Angeles as well as television programs covering the World Cup of Football in Mexico (1986), Italy (1990) and the U.S. (1994).

The mass media interest in sport is rooted in the huge power it continues to exert on the public (even though I cannot say how much longer it will be able to keep it up!). This power is called "popular passion", a phenomenon which has a crucial influence on the circulation figures of magazines and newspapers, attracting press advertisements, determining the success of a broadcast and – through audience ratings – attracting the interest of radio and TV commercial advertisers.

Without venturing into areas that have nothing to do strictly with my responsibilities, such as the newspaper industry – even though even there the situation is not very different from my own industry – I would like to draw your attention to something with which I am more qualified to deal: soccer and television. I think that the present scenario in this respect is alarming, to say the least! First of all, we have to admit that in recent years the "soccer system" has found a way to earn the maximum possible financial resources by selling the "soccer product" in thousands of small "packages". And all this has been done in defiance of the Italians' passion for the sport which, until just recently, used to be considered the most beautiful game in the world.

This marketing tactic – we are told by the experts – has produced a wide range of television offerings that are very difficult for the public to assimilate, creating incredible confusion with so many matches being played, in addition to "overdosing" on midweek matches (Series B matches, as well as European tournaments) that cram the television schedule full, seven days a week.

There is far too much soccer! And it is no longer a big deal to buy the broadcasting rights for the "first screening" of the Sunday Series A matches for EUR 61 million a year. People are now getting bored with it. The market has ignored its most elementary rules: it has flooded and oversupplied the market, leading to public "indigestion". And the quality of the entertainment is becoming increasingly tawdry, except when the usual well-established clubs continue to fight it out with each other – the clubs that have no financial problems, that can afford to invest huge fortunes, because they are the property of great multinationals.

I go along with those who criticise people that keep harking back too much to the past, because we have to move forward. But there are times when the past can offer extraordinary examples. Years ago in Italy, many of us used to follow a fixed Sunday ritual with great punctually. It began with Sunday morning Mass, followed by the rush to the nearest pastry shop (there is always one near every church), then quickly back home for the Sunday family lunch, and immediately afterwards a walk to the football stadium to see the game, after which we would go rush back home to watch *"90th Minute"* programme presented by Paolo Valenti, who very adroitly avoided ever giving away the results of the game of which excerpts (usually the second half) were broadcast immediately after his legendary programme. Yes, those were certainly the days in which there were still professionals around who knew how to convey not only the thrills of sport, but also its values, and who used the media with sound common sense according to clear-cut rules and with proper respect for a very "powerful" instrument: the microphone. There was still a taste for entertainment. Sport was practised above all as a game, without neglecting its educational side. But today we have given way to the rules of the market, and we are culpably ignoring the educational and informational role of our media.

Sport today has certainly become richer (not only soccer, but other disciplines are also discovering new ways of making big money that was unthinkable even a few years ago, thanks to television and sponsorships) – richer in terms of money, that is, but significantly poorer in terms of values!

I will not go into the daily reports of the negative sides of soccer, which still remains Italy's most popular sport, even though the TV audience ratings show that other disciplines broadcast at the last Olympic Games are surprisingly and encouragingly gaining in popularity with viewers; but I would like to speak about the responsibility that I feel I can attribute to the news, and particularly the people running the news industry: the publishers, those responsible for radio and television broadcasts, and the press.

Today, society is increasingly losing the sense of human values. The dash for success seems to be the only way of demonstrating a life lived with commitment. Sport, too, as the mirror of the reality in which we live, offers examples that are not always positive. The myth of wealth has permeated through to every area of human activity, causing people to lose the perception of what is right and what is wrong. Everything now goes, in the name of success. Which means wealth.

What is the role of the media in all this? They report, inform, and denounce, but they certainly do not educate! The quality of the programmes shown on television is declining all the time. Judging from my own experience I can safely say that the expectations of the viewing public are also very low, and tend to be turned off by educational programmes, mostly preferring programmes with very little cultural content such as reality shows or wrestling matches- the epitome of phoney sports- to programmes that debate issues similar to those we are discussing at this seminar.

Let me conclude by harking back, for a moment, to the little soccer pitches we used to have in the parish 'oratory' clubs, where the parish priest organised matches that went on and on interminably, until dusk fell, often ending with no winners and no losers. Those parish clubs produced "little champions". Those experiences helped us to mature, because it enabled us to acquire real life values that included respect for others, knowing how to win fairly and without pushing victory to extremes and to accept defeat graciously. And I would also like to make a very personal request to the Church: give us again our parish sport clubs! Give us again parish priests who, with referee's whistle and an eye for discipline, are not afraid of getting their shoes dirty on the pitch in order to be with the youth of their parish. Priest who are capable of giving them formation in virtues and discipline through games and sport.

I am certain that the value of sport is handed on through such healthy, genuine relations as these, even if they may be considered by some to be somewhat out of fashion today.

Sport and doping

PASQUALE BELLOTTI*

Doping is a dramatic phenomenon that not only destroys the essence of sport at its very roots, but also undermines the very values of society.[1] It is also a serious bioethical issue because drug-use places people's health in jeopardy and in many cases compromises the very lives of the athletes. We can therefore say without any hesitation that it boils down to an issue of protecting human life.[2]

I will begin by listing some of the factors that have given rise to doping and continue to fuel this social scourge. Then, we will consider why it is becoming increasingly more urgent to marshal the efforts of those in authority to publicly acknowledge and consequently overcome such failures as the reluctance to take any notice, the indifference and the incompetence of those who contribute to the spread of doping in order to suit their own purposes or interests.

The number of people who have recourse to doping continues to grow. Conservative estimates by Libra indicate that, in Italy alone, 400,000 people were habitual drug users in sport in 2003; this rose to 450,000 in 2004; and to over 500,000 in 2005. It has also been shown that doping is becoming increasingly common even in the very poor

* Doctor Pasquale Bellotti holds degrees in Philosophy and Medicine. Formerly with the Sports School of the Italian National Olympics Committee (CONI), he now lectures at "La Sapienza" University of Rome, and the Institute of Motor Science in Rome. He recently began studying for a PhD in Bioethics and Doping at the Pontifical Athenaeum Regina Apostolorum.

[1] M. ATTALI (editor), *Le sport et ses valeurs*, La Dispute/Snédit, Paris 2004.

[2] P. BELLOTTI, G. BENZI, *Farmaci, allenamento e sport*, Il Pensiero Scientifico Editore, Roma 1990 (cf. capitoli 1 e 4); P. BELLOTTI, *Il doping: storia, sostanze, effetti, aspettative, danni. Quali discipline, quali personalità, quale morale*, in Movimento, Anno 5, n. 3, 1989, 165-167.

111

countries. Experts think that this increase is primarily due to the commercialisation of sport: financial reward is now the rule, and earnings are rising all the time. The incentive of huge earnings, coupled by the economic and financial interests of their entourage, force athletes to continually step up the pace in order to achieve victory. In other words, it seems that the sporting world itself is inducing athletes to take performance enhancing drugs in order to meet the great expectations of others and has led to what many people call a "doping-prone environment".[3]

The incredible diffusion of doping creates multiple problems in its wake which are unfortunately linked to a certain malignant will, and in many cases hypocrisy, on the part of those working in the sports industry and making their money from it. For it is hard to believe that it is so hard to detect those athletes who use illegal substances, which almost inevitably fall into three well-known categories: 41% anabolic steroids, 28.6% growth hormones (including EPO in 14.3% of cases) and 16.7% stimulants.

Neither can we say that we know everything about doping. In fact, doping is extremely dangerous precisely because we still know very little about the new frontiers it is opening. For example, we have no idea about the quantities of drugs being taken by athletes (which are far in excess of the levels recommended for therapeutic use), or the "mixtures" of different substances (usually ones that have never been tested for medical purposes), the length of time they are taken (which, if excessive, can have serious repercussions on the body), and the collateral effects caused by the interaction of different drugs (which can often be lethal, as the newspaper headlines frequently confirm).

[3] The European Commission, which is running its own institutional campaign to combat doping in sport has embarked on a study of the structural causes that explain the increase in doping in sport. The Directorate-General for Education and Cultural of the Commission therefore commissioned KPMG Economic Consulting (KPMG EC) and the Asser Institute to analyse the socio-economic causes of doping. The long report produced by KPMG and the Asser Institute was based on a wide-ranging survey, extensive research of the most authoritative writings on the subject, and numerous interviews with experts in the world of sport, marketing, mass media and healthcare.

What is even much more alarming is the fact that doping no longer involves only a few of the leading athletes, but now it extends to the new and extremely young athletes who are just entering the world of sport. So the question we have to ask at this point is, why we cannot stop the increase in doping? Who are the people responsible for it, and who are contributing to spreading its practice? First of all, it has to be publicly admitted that there are serious shortcomings in anti-doping monitoring which up until now are performed by testing urine samples. Not only are these urine tests unreliable, but they are carried out before competitions, whereas they ought to be performed during the athletes' training period when they are more likely to have taken banned drugs and substances. Furthermore, when we talk about doping we have to acknowledge that this involves a cultural problem. For it is often the parents of children who practise sport who conspire with this medicalisation of sport by asking their doctors for vitamins and food supplements that they see advertised, but these should not be used lightly. On the other hand, it is of no help in the battle against doping that doctors and trainers – those who ought to play a leading role in toppling the false myths on which sport is being built – remain silent out of self-interest or for their own convenience.

Sponsors are also guilty of encouraging doping by exerting constant pressure on their endorsed players to perform since profits depend on their success. The 1999 European Union Conference on Sport spoke out very forcefully in this regard, by saying that "The fight should be targeted more at the real causes that contribute to the proliferation of doping. Drug culture and permissiveness, excessive competition, unduly high stakes, pressure from sponsors – commercial and/or institutional – should all be rejected".[4]

In the final analysis, the mass media are also responsible for this indifference and for neglecting this serious social problem. There is

[4] See the "Conclusions of the First European Union Conference on Sport" held in Olympia (Greece), 20-23 May 1999. Document can be found in Asser Institute archives at: www.sportslaw.nl/categorieen/intro.asp?sub_categorie=40.

very serious misinformation regarding doping issues, and the results of surveys and investigations conducted by law enforcement agencies are often not publicised. Apparently, they are not "newsworthy"! Meanwhile, European statistics over the past five years show that millions of doses of EPO have been seized in Cyprus, 2.5 tonnes of steroids in Vienna, massive quantities of GH, EPO, anabolic steroids and stimulants in Barcelona and Brussels, 13 million doses of doping substances in Madrid and surrounding provinces.

In light of all of this, we can therefore see that what is missing above all is a genuine training in sportsmanship that pursues the values for which sport can be a vehicle and which educates young athletes to give the best of themselves though the type of training that is at the service and needs of the human person. Instead, the only objective that is offered to the athletes is that of winning, cost what it may.

Before the threat of doping, who has the duty to do something about it? Primary responsibility certainly lies with governments, who are supposed to enact robust laws to wipe out doping and promote clean sport. It would be appropriate for governments to ratify the agreements on international monitoring. The 1999 European Union Conference on Sport, held in Olympia, revealed that illegal doping in sport is on the increase. It went on to declare that the illegal production and trafficking of anabolic steroids has now become a law enforcement concern, and many countries have already changed their criminal law in order to prosecute these crimes. If this work is to be effective- the document stated- coordination must be improved between governments, police forces and customs authorities.[5]

In addition to the national sports institutions (Ministry of Sport, National Olympics Committees, sports federations etc) which need great determination to address this problem, a major contribution can also be made by such international institutions as the International

---

[5] *Ibid*; for additional arguments see the European Council's *European Sports Charter* and the *Code of Sports Ethics,* http://www.sportdevelopment.org.uk/European_sports_charter__revised_.pdf

Olympics Committee (IOC) which recently made doping the fourth main current problem (joining gigantism, nationalism and corruption),[6] and the World Anti-Doping Agency (WADA) that was created in 1999.

But the struggle against doping is not only the responsibility of governments and public institutions. All those who are involved in sport must help to solve the problem. According to experts,[7] it is necessary to fully acquaint athletes, players and every person involved (parents, teachers, managers, physicians, etc) with the real dangers of using doping substances and with the results of epidemiological surveys on the long-term health of athletes; financial resources and appropriate technical tools must be supplied to the authorities responsible for controlling the substances that currently exist on the market; it must be made mandatory to introduce markers in doping drugs to facilitate their detection in anti-doping tests; the sports system must be rendered independent of the authorities responsible for carrying out checks and controls, so that they can work in total independence; in every sports discipline, the fixtures and calendars must be thinned out; rigorous and inflexible ethical rules must be enforced by sports medicine and its specialists; a general debate must be taken up regarding the ramifications of the world of sports' "quest for top performance", and we have to take note of the fact that there are always huge financial interests that are underlying doping. In summary, we must promote a healthy vision of sport that extends beyond the sole goal of peak performance and is fully cognisant that the use of drugs in sport not only threatens the health of individuals but also negates the dignity of the person and the possibility of establishing genuine human relations.

---

[6] See the following IOC document: *Report of the IOC 2000 Commission, made at the 110ᵗʰ IOC Session, December 1999, Lusanne* which can be found at www.olympic.org.

[7] See B. HOULIHAN, *Dying to win – Doping in sport and the development of anti-doping policy,* Council of Europe Publishing, Strasbourg 1999.

II. ROUND TABLE

Sport: frontier of the new evangelisation

INTRODUCTION

NORBERT MÜLLER *

A s Paul VI observed, "the split between the gospel and culture is without a doubt the drama of our time".[1] In fact, especially when we consider many of the forms of today's entertainment culture, the gap between these and the gospel can seem abysmal. Yet, at the same time, when we look for a way of bridging this gap, sport emerges to the forefront as a phenomena with unique possibilities. The many problems that plague the world of sport were made evident in yesterday's panel discussion. Yet, in spite of these problems, sport, as an activity that engages millions of people on a daily basis, can offer a door by which the gospel can penetrate our culture. It is in this sense that it can be considered a "frontier of the new evangelization", a place of encounter with the gospel message with those people- especially the youth- who may be far away from the Church. Not only can sport provide an opportunity for evangelization, but it may also bear fruit in the field of ecumenism and provide opportunities for inter-religious dialogue.

We must not underestimate the treasure of our faith and how it imbues the way Catholic sports are perceived, practiced and played. As a professor of sport, some years ago I directed the thesis of a gradu-

---

* Professor Müller teaches sport at the University of Joannes Guttenburg in Mainz, Germany. As a member of The Commission for Culture and Education of the International Olympic Committee (IOC), he has attended all of the Olympic games since 1972 with the exception of Moscow. In 1999, Prof. Müller was one of the independent experts involved in the restructuring of the IOC after the scandal of Salt Lake City. He has been vice president of Unesco's International Fairplay Commission and president of the Pier de Coubertin International Commitee. Since 1974, he has served as a member of the Church and Sport Scientific Commmitte within the German Catholic Bishop's Conference.

[1] PAUL VI, Apostolic Exhortation *Evangelii Nuntiandi*, n. 20.

ate student who was educated under communism without any contact with Christianity. She decided to do her thesis on the education perspectives in the work of the French Dominican Rev. Henri Didon. (It was Fr. Didon who introduced Pier de Coubertin to the phrase: *Citius, altius, fortius* which he would adopt for the Olympics.) After a year of reading the writings and sermons of Fr. Didon, she wrote and defended her thesis. A few months after her defence, she invited me to her baptism; and one year later, to her Catholic wedding mass. She found Jesus Christ through her studies of sport through the eyes of a Christian author!

A foremost field of evangelization of the world of sport lies in that of education. Catholic schools can play a major role in the practice and promotion of a sport ethos rooted in the spirit of Christian education and in close cooperation with the family. This premise, however, assumes that Catholic teachers, including physical education teachers, coaches and youth directors, are aware of the contribution they can make to "teach" ethical and sport values at the grass roots level.

On the other hand we find the significant role of professional athletes: those truly extraordinary athletes who manage to combine a high level of performance with a high ethical standard can become outstanding role models who are able to manage well the ample resonance they receive from the mass media. Religious symbols transmitted by athletes, like the sign of the cross, have also been playing an increasingly important role at large media sporting events in recent years. They can be seen as signs of benediction, but they can also may convey for some a sense of superstition.

The Christian faith urges us to oppose the idolatry of the body as well as any possible exploitation of the person and should motivate sportsmen and sportswomen to stand up for fairness, tolerance and solidarity. Catholic sport associations can play an important role in influencing the everyday practice of sport if they take their Christian moral values seriously, and reflect these values in their policies and procedures.

For Christians, sport can also be seen as a ministry to the weak and segregated. Through sport, people can gain new hope and may return or be re-integrated into the community. Families, parishes and sports clubs are all called upon to develop a new "culture of Sunday" that is truly a celebration of "The Lord's Day" through an appropriate arrangement of events. Sport schedules have to be reconsidered in order to make it possible for families and youth, as well as professional athletes to take part in the celebration of the Sunday Mass.

Religious services could also be offered at major sport events. A proven form of the Church's presence at these national and international events like the Olympic Games, the Paralympics and the World Championships is the so-called 'sport chaplain'. It is often the case that such a pastoral ministry, often realized in an ecumenical spirit of collaboration, reaches not only believers but also those who are aloof from the Church.

The relations between the Church and secular sport organizations are not always free from occasional tension. Nevertheless, the multitude of common interests and aims calls for a continuous and progressive cooperation with each other. All those working in national and international sport organizations can bear fruit when they allow their actions to be motivated by Christian principles. These efforts can be further enhanced by joint committees, and joint activities and conferences with representatives from the various sports teams and associations at the international, national, local, and parish level.

In order to carry out this "new-evangelization" a coordinated effort is needed among all these sporting "frontiers". I believe that the initial investment at the vertex- that of coordination and organization- can yield a high return at the base. Yet, each individual and sport institution has a significant role to play in building this bridge between the gospel and today's culture. Let us now listen to what the panellist have to say about their particular frontier.

Catholic sport associations

Catholic sports organisations, like the two large European associations represented at this seminar (FICEP and FISEC), began to exist at the end of the 19th century and beginning of the 20th century as parish initiatives similar to civic sports associations. In a certain sense, these Catholic associations are a fruit of the Encyclical *Rerum novarum* (1891) of Leo XIII, renewed a hundred years later by John Paul II with *Centesimus annus*. Although *Rerum novarum* does not concern sport directly, it regards something very connected to sport as it deals with the world of work and leisure time. It was specifically during the period of this important papal document that parishes began to attend more directly to their youth and proposed sporting activities as an effective means for their development. We also cannot deny that the values promoted in sport are, and will remain to be, human and Christian values.

The *Fédération International Education Physique et sportive* (FICEP) was born in 1906 as an initiative of the French Catholic Sporting Federation (FGSPF) and of the Catholic Italian Sports Federation (FASCI). When these two federations were gathered together for an international gymnastic competition, they launched the idea of uniting all Catholic sports associations under one international organization. In 1908, Pius X gave impetus to this project by receiving in the Vatican's inner court-

* Clément Schertzinger, a native of the province of Neuf-Brisach in France, is the actual president of the Fédération International Education Physique et sportive (FICEP) that was founded in Nancy at the beginning of the 20th century. Mr. Schertzinger is also honorary president of FSCF, the national French member of FICEP. Today, FICEP has about 3.5 million members in 12 European countries as well as Cameron and Madagascar. Schertzinger has frequently been a delegate of the Holy See to various meetings regarding sport related themes of the UNESCO or the European Union.

yard the participants of the first ever International Competition of Catholic Gymnastics and sports. During this event, in which more that 2000 athletes took part from around the world, the Pope expressed his desire that this new federation "be extended in as much as the Catholic Church is extended, in order that all be united in one spirit and one heart in one and the same endeavour".[1]

In 1913 there took place in Rome the first great sporting event of FICEP. Although activities were interrupted from 1914 to 1918 due to World War I, they were taken up again in 1919 with the arrival of peace. Association membership grew quickly in the years between 1922 and 1939, with a sports competition in Paris in 1923, Prague in 1929, Antwerp in 1930, Vienna in 1936 and Ljubljana in 1938 which brought together thousands of youth who delighted in participating in these sporting activities which were characterized by an atmosphere of friendship and Christian competition. With World War II, FICEP activities were suspended and taken up again with greater difficulty after the war. In fact, Socialistic nationalism, and later, communism would dismantle these Catholic sport federations, in particular in Eastern Europe, where the federations were only able to begin again after the fall of the Berlin wall in 1989.

Today, FICEP is an international sports federation that seeks to educate youth in human and Christian values through sporting and recreational youth activities. FICEP promotes the mutual exchange of experiences of people of different cultures, traditions, and backgrounds by gathering youth together from different countries for international events. Convinced of the strong formative value of sporting, artistic, and recreational activities as a means to foster virtue, FICEP seeks the overall development of the physical, moral, human and social faculties of its members through these activities which are grounded in and inspired by the teachings of the Gospel. To facilitate these objectives, FISEC is

---

[1] Pius X, *To the participants of the International competition of Gymnastics and Sports*, September 27, 1908 [our translation]. Original Italian text can be found in G.B. Gandolfo-L. Vassallo (editors), *Lo sport nei documenti pontifici*, La Scuola, Brescia 1994, 19.

assisted by a youth commission that focuses on human development, a pastoral commission that attends to their spiritual formation, and a sports commission that organizes the annual FICEP games.

Based on my years of experience in the field of sport, and within the perspective of the "new evangelization" to which all of us are protagonists, I am convinced that sport can provide a useful means of responding to the educational needs of the youth of today. Certainly it is not as easy task, above all in a society which continues to rapidly evolve. Yet recalling the beginnings of our International association, our history can teach us that, in spite of difficulties, we can indeed make progress and arrive at a better future. I continue to have faith that we can reach our goals.

To conclude, I would like to recall the words that John Paul II addressed to participants of the General Assembly of FICEP in 1986 on occasion of our 75th anniversary. Regarding the role of sport in an age of growing leisure time, he observed: "It is in this context that the human values of sport appear clearest. It is seen as a worthwhile way of using one's time, because in sport man acquires greater self-mastery and manifests a fitting expression of the dominion of his intelligence and will over his body. Whence arises a serene attitude of respect, esteem and redemption for sporting activity, and as a consequence its consideration as a possible occasion of ennoblement. May you consider your mission an important effort to bring it about that, with the proliferation of sports activity at the collective level, a "redemption", so to speak, of the sports phenomenon take place, according to the principles always proclaimed by the Church. May every athlete strive to attain, through self-mastery, those basic human virtues that constitute a balanced personality, and that likewise develop a grateful and humble attitude towards the Giver of every good, and thus physical health as well, in this way opening up the soul to the horizons of faith".[2]

---

[2] JOHN PAUL II, *Address to FICEP: Sports can help spread fraternity and peace,* "L'Osservatore Romano" Weekly English Edition, n. 17, April 28, 1986, 5.

Christian presence in sporting institutions

ARTURO SALAH*

In light of what has been said so far regarding the strong secularization of our age, I would like to reflect on our responsibility as Catholics engaged in the world of sport. In what ways can we be more present in this world and take better advantage of those aspects of sporting activity that ennoble the person, motivate people to give their best and foster the development of such virtues as fortitude, solidarity, honesty, unity, and mutual respect? In *Evangelii nuntiandi,* Paul VI invited the laity "to put to use every Christian and evangelical possibility latent but already present and active in the affairs of the world".[1] Without a doubt, one such possibility is that of sport.

I would like to now briefly share with you some of my experiences of a Christian presence in sports institutions as a former player, professional coach, and as the Undersecretary for Sport in my country, Chile. Through my years of coaching professional soccer, I have been able to witness a marked religious tendency in the players. This was often characterized by expressions of popular piety more than a deep-seated faith. Yet, such customs as making the sign of the cross before entering the field, or displaying religious images in the locker room, or invoking God's help in moments of tension or difficulty, are clear signs of a desire to make God present in their daily lives.

* Arturo Salah was born in Chile in 1955 and is married with four children. He played professional soccer for fifteen years before beginning a career in coaching. He has coached professionally for such first division teams in Chile as Colo-Colo, Catholic University, and The University of Chile. From1990-1993, Mr. Salah was the technical director of the Chilean national team and from 1994-1997 he coached the 1rst division Monterrey Soccer Club in Mexico. He also has served as the Vice-minister of sport in the Chilean government. Presently, he is the technical director of Huachipato first division soccer team in Talcahuano, Chile.
[1] PAUL VI, *Apostolic Exhortation Evangelii nuntiandi*, n. 70.

One interesting initiative that manifests the great religious senti-ments of the Latin American people was that of "Hosanna", a third division soccer team started by an evangelical pastor and a group of former professional players. "Hosanna" had the custom of gifting their opponents with a copy of the gospel and to make an effort dur-ing the game not to commit fouls nor use foul language. Their mission was also shared by the "Hosanna" fans who encouraged their team by singing spiritual and liturgical hymns during the match. Certainly no one can deny the originality of this initiative, even if they were often laughed at or jeered by their opponents. Nonetheless, it remains a valid example of a concrete effort to witness to the gospel in profes-sional sport.

Another experience I fondly recall was my work as the responsible for student formation at the Pontifical University of Chile which has one of the most prestigious sports associations of the country. I was able to work closely with a young Catholic priest who, as chaplain, often celebrated mass for the students and had a great rapport with them. I was impressed by the zeal of this priest who, while being a great fan of sport, became a spiritual father and a constant religious presence in the lives of these young people. Because he participated in their daily activities and shared in their passion for sport, he was able to establish a sincere friendship with the students that allowed him to naturally attend to their spiritual questions and their interest in their faith which arose spontaneously.

For three years, I had the opportunity to direct one the profes-sional soccer clubs in Mexico. During this time, I was surprised to dis-cover that nearly all of the major stadiums and training centres in Mexico had a chapel. For the Mexican people, having a physical place like a chapel within the these structures is seen as something quite normal. So much so that many players have the habit of making a visit to the chapel before every game. I wanted to bring this interesting opportunity to our attention in order for us to consider what types of worship spaces or ecumenical chapels are provided for at world sport-ing events today. This assistance to the players and the fans could be a way to counteract the negative aspects that sport suffers today and to enrich these great sporting events such as the Olympics or the World Cup which hold claim to the promotion of human values and attract the attention of the entire world.

The affirmation of Christian values in sport is an achievable goal, given that these values are inherent to healthy sport activity. For example, we can reflect on the unifying potential that major sports events have to assemble nations, peoples and generations in a unique meeting point and offers opportunity for dialogue between different countries, races and religions. Today, the challenge of contemporary culture is that of being able to promote a concept of sport that responds to the demands of our times without distorting its ethical foundation. We must consider the concrete ways we can restore these values to ordinary life and give them meaning in a society where individualism, utilitarianism and hedonism prevail. It is not simply a question of not committing fouls in a game or of singing religious hymns in a stadium. Rather, it is a question of enabling sports to follow the "right criteria" so that they become "a school of honesty, courage, endurance, perseverance and fraternity"[2] as John Paul II stressed in a meeting with soccer players from the national teams of Italy and Argentina.

In order to reach these objectives, it seems to me that those who work with athletes have a fundamental role to play. Often, those of us who have athletes under our care are only concerned with developing technical skills and offering rigorous training so that their physical capacities can provide peak performance. Yet, a Christian presence in sport is exercised in great part in the unique relationship between coach and player. It is the coach who can assist the players in order to give meaning to their activities so that the discipline of sport helps them develop as a complete person. This task is exercised day by day, in between the lines of their conversation with the athletes. It consists in an unwritten pedagogy that is best communicated by one's example.

[2] JOHN PAUL II, *Address to Italian and Argentine Athletes*, May 25, 1979 [our translation]. Original text can be found in "Insegnamenti di Giovanni Paolo II" (1979) II, 1216.

In order for a coach or trainer to become a true teacher he must transmit to his players that which transcends his particular discipline. A true teacher educates not simply with his of her words, but also with their deeds. Likewise, a coach will be a leader for his players if there is coherence between what he says, what he does, and who he is.

These same points hold true as well for those who direct sports institutions. How important it is that the leaders of sports institutions, associations, and federations, are people who are committed to the values of sport and its potential to elevate the human person. Sooner or later, those who want to see sport practiced according to its noble ideas have to confront a sport that has been politicized or is no longer in accordance with the positive values of sport.

I conclude by recalling that appeal of Paul VI to put to use every possibility that is within our reach. During the Jubilee for Sport, John Paul II reinforced this by expressing his desire that managers, technicians and athletes "find new creative and motivating zeal through sports that knows how, in a constructive spirit, to reconcile the complex demands made by the current cultural and social changes with the unchangeable requirements of the human being".[3] For all of us engaged in the world of sport, I retain that one of the most effective ways of evangelizing this field is by the testimony of the coherence of our lives in word, being and action.

---

[3] JOHN PAUL II, *Homily at the Jubilee for the Word of Sport: Even the greatest champions need Christ*, "L'Osservatore Romano" Weekly English Edition, n. 44, November 1, 2000, 1.

Professional sport chaplains

FORTUNATO FREZZA*

I will seek to touch upon, even if only in general, two points that are at the root of our theme. The first regards the competitive spirit which in a certain sense is a social characteristic that distinguishes the human person of our time in the way they conduct their social relations. The second point directly concerns the personal environment in which we find the professional athlete today. This reflection is rooted not only in my experiences as a chaplain of a professional soccer team, that of S.S. Roma, but also from my years as a parish priest and as a biblical scholar.

Competition is essential to the human condition. From the beginning of human history, man has needed to "compete" with all of the natural threats of the climate and his environmental surroundings in order to survive. The spirit of competition can be found in all human activities and is certainly a positive and indispensable drive that enables the person to develop their capacities and succeed in their endeavours by overcoming the various challenges that confront them.

When this basic habit of competing is applied to the activities that pertain to the category of *ludus*, or games, the sporting phenomenon is revealed. True and healthy competition which generates great challenge, is the very soul and root of sport. Because of this, if there was not the possibility of competition, there would not be sport. This applies to both individual sport where one seeks to overcome one's

---

* Msgr. Frezza was born in Rome but grew up in Viterbo where he served as a parish priest for eighteen years. During that time, he competed for more than 10 federal soccer championships with his parish team. Msgr. Frezza is also a professor of sacred scripture and presently works in the Vatican as the undersecretary for the Synod of bishops. Since 1986, he has been chaplain to the professional soccer team, "Roma".

personal record as well as competitive social sport where at least two people confront each other in a specific discipline. Yet, even though competition is in itself a favourable characteristic of an athlete as it seeks self-improvement, today it runs the risk of devolution.

In the professional sports environment, competition is not contained only in the desire to confront oneself or the other, which will always be a fundamental aspect of healthy sport- but it becomes influenced by the strong economic interests of the sport industry that often relentlessly seek the greatest financial success possible. Entering more profoundly into the dynamics behind professional sport, one finds unfortunately, evidence of corruption, or a certain contamination from external elements. So, how can a sports chaplain confront this threat of contamination? Perhaps the simplest and most direct way is to be committed to revealing the true face of sport, which is above all the work of human effort. We must not forget that an athlete is one who is truly dedicated, accustomed to arduous training and self sacrifice. Certainly this contamination of the word of sport exists, and a real effort is needed to eliminate it, but it must go beyond denouncing scandal or worse still, becoming discouraged. For on the other hand, even before sport became "professional" there have existed these negative elements along side it. In fact, in a homily from the second century considers the effort and discipline of an athlete as a metaphor for perseverance in the Christian faith. Here the author states that if anyone *corrumpit, aufertur et extra stadium eicitur*, that is, if anyone seeks recourse to cheating in order to attain victory let them be disqualified and expulsed from the stadium.

The second point I would like to touch on is something that although it does not directly involve my work as a chaplain, certainly conditions it in a great degree. I would like to reflect on the original environment from which all athletes have their beginning. Christian athletes are born in and raised in the surroundings of a family, a school, and a parish, which are the essential places where the formation of the person begins to take shape. Because of this, the role of a sports chaplain consists in building upon, in most cases, a work that has already begun. In the majority of cases it is the family that represents the environment in which a passion for sport is fed and encouraged. Because of this, the family plays an irreplaceable role in the future development of an athlete as the place where a child's basic concept of what sport is and how it should be played is formed. Parents have a great responsibility of transmitting to their children who play sport a just sense of competition. Regarding this, allow me to express my dismay at a certain erroneous tendency on the part of those parents who consider their child as a future champion and subject their child to conditions of living that are based on their false expectations and do not respond to reality and coerce their child into thinking that they have to reach victory at all costs.

Schools are another formative environment where children are taught not only basic learning skills, but also how to deal with others and their social environment through their studies but also through play and especially through sport. Through the education they receive in the school children are able to grasp the human aspect of sport. These are aspects that are not linked to the professional sport environment, but rather, the very exercise of sport itself is the means by which such values and habits such as honesty, courage, perseverance, self-improvement, discipline, and team work are conveyed.

To end, I would like to suggest that along side of schools and sports associations, one of the best places where the youth can develop these virtues and receive a personal assistance towards their integral development is the parish oratory. Perhaps what is most needed in the athletes of today is precisely this: a complete education of the whole person, body and soul. Yet in the parish oratory attention is given to developing all of one's faculties! Yes, their athletic and intellectual capacities are engaged in the oratory, but also their spiritual faculties are harmonious cultivated alongside these through prayer and the liturgy.

Olympic chaplains

Bernhard Maier*

There are two aspects relevant to this panel discussion that come to mind in light of my personal experiences from working with Olympic athletes. The first regards something external- the general conditions that determine my work when exercising my role as a chaplain to the Austrian Olympic team. The second regards those personal qualities and dispositions that I think are necessary for a Olympic chaplain to be effective in his ministry. I would like to offer these suggestions in the hope that they might be useful for those who work with professional athletes.

In 1972, the Austrian National Olympic Committee accepted the proposal of the Catholic Church in Austria to provide a priest as a chaplain to the Olympic team. This began a very positive relationship between the Church and the State in Austria within the field of professional sport and has greatly facilitated my work ever since. In fact, the work of the Church in the field of sport in Austria extends beyond the Olympics to the world of youth where we find at the diocesan level, the so called, "sporting communities". These places provided for by the Church where children can come and practice different sports are very much appreciated by the entire community. There is also an office for "Church and sport" within the Bishop's Conference of Austria

* Rev. Bernhard Maier was ordained a priest for the Salesians in 1978. He has a doctorate in Sports Sciences. Since 1984, he has been the chaplain of the Austrian Olympic team and since 2000, his responsibilities also include being chaplain to the Paralympics. Father Maier is a member of the directive committee of the first division soccer championship in Germany, and has also been chaplain at the World Cup of soccer. He has authored several books about sport including a series on "Sport, Ethics and Religion". From 1995 to the present, he is the director of the Don Bosco Gymnasium in Unterwaltersdorf (Vienna).

that enables the Church to be in contact with and present within the various sport associations in Austria.

Regarding the qualities of an Olympic chaplain, I would like to outline some points and give some tips that are based on my interacting with athletes over the past twenty three years. First of all, I think that an Olympic chaplain needs to be well grounded in his knowledge about sports in general, and it is best if he himself practices a sport as well. He needs to possess a genuine interest in his field and in the athletes with who he attends. He should seek to be present at their competitions and showing a real interest in their lives and those concerns and pressures which they face. Without manifesting a genuine interest in their lives of these athletes, it will be difficult to win their confidence. His interest should go beyond minimal requirements, and should include visiting the athletes when they are sick or injured, or when they have other needs. In a word, he should become a good shepherd for his team and those entrusted to his care.

My pastoral work as a chaplain has not always been easy. I have often encountered obstacles, especially in my efforts to establishing and maintaining a good rapport with the athletes. Because of this great flexibility is needed, whether it refers to scheduling liturgical functions, or other moments of encounter, in order to accommodate the hectic and very demanding personal schedules of the athletes as well as so many various factors that come into play during the Olympics in order to seek and arrive at what is best for the entire team. One needs to know how to accept disappointments and failures that are bound to occur and to be tenacious in order to keep on going. A chaplain must also have the courage to offer and promote religious services while at the same time exercising discretion and prudence. Lastly, perhaps one of the most important points is that a chaplain is well prepared in order to promote a Christian sport ethic that is convincing, being well grounded in reason and that is capable of opening up a door to the spiritual level and those themes that regard our faith.

To end, I would like to recall the valid contribution the lay faithful are called to make in this field. In my work as a sport's chaplain, lay people have been very instrumental in enabling me to establish contact with sports associations and with professional sport teams. This is a valid point not to be overlooked.

6 Pastoral work and major sporting events

Pastoral work and major sporting events

HANS-GERD SCHÜTT*

G iven the social situation and the principles regulating the relationship of Church and State in the Federal Republic of Germany,
there are numerous fields of cooperation between the Catholic Church
in Germany and German sports federations. Organized sport in Germany is represented by the German Sports Federation (Deutscher
Sportbund), by specialized federations as well as the National
Olympic Committee and the National Paralympic Committee. The
Church is represented by both the Catholic Sports Association known
as the "Deutsche Jugend Kraft" (DJK) with currently 520,000 members organised into 1170 clubs, and by the Sports Commissioner of the
German Bishops' Conference- which is my title. The Sports Commissioner's functions include providing pastoral guidance at major sporting events, such as the Olympic Games, the subsequent Paralympics,
the FIFA World Cup next year in Germany, and other national and
international sporting events.

Both the Catholic Church in Germany and the Evangelical Church
send a chaplain or a pastor to accompany the Olympic teams and provide pastoral guidance. During the Olympic Games in Athens, for
example, pastoral work included the classical pastoral care activities
such as the celebration of mass, daily prayers, personal talks as well as
pastoral care of the sick. Pastoral service was not limited to the ath-

* Rev. Hans-Gerd Schütt was ordained a priest for the diocese of Aachen in 1987. In
1990 he was appointment diocesan councilor of the Catholic sport association "Deutsche
Jugend Kraft" (DJK) and in 1996 he became the national councilor of the DJK, which has
over 500,000 members nationwide. In 1999, he was appointed the commissioner of the
"Church and sport" office of the German Bishop's Conference and has also been chaplain
to the German Olympic team in Los Angeles and Athens.

letes, but was also offered to German coaches and officials as well as journalists, doctors and basically to everyone who had come to Athens with the German team. This pastoral care was fully supported by the Olympic organizers, which meant that we were fully accredited, we were involved in team briefings and in official appearances of the Olympic team, we received logistic and moral support, and we were involved in the preparation of the Olympic Games at an early stage.

In general, pastoral guidance and missionary presence of the Church are of particular significance and is a visible sign that the Church is an integral part of society and that it, in fulfilment of its mission, takes an interest in the lives of all people, including athletes. The Church clearly proves that it does not withdraw to an inside world, but that it is sent out into the world to proclaim the Gospel in a self-confident and dynamic – yet non aggressive – way, and in a special situation. For quite a few of these people, this is the first contact after a long time with the Church. And for some non-Christians, this is their first ever contact with the Church. In this way, the Church has the opportunity to show that one can look at life from another angle, where one's source of hope goes beyond their immediate life. Professional and Olympic athletes can often feel left all alone in their search for the spiritual, especially when coaches or trainers neglect this aspect altogether. For this reason, sport chaplains can help athletes to make a connection between their intense experiences of a major sporting event- with all the related challenges, extreme situations, triumphs, defeats and various other experiences- on the one hand, and their questions concerning the deeper meaning and purpose of life, on the other hand. Often, athletes will tell us: "Your presence here shows us that the Church takes an interest in what we do". Therefore this outreach should not be underestimated. In fact, this proves that sport is an evolving sphere of pastoral activity for the Church that can provide new opportunities previously unknown.

Given the denominational situation in Germany, sports chaplains are offered an effective and excellent area of ecumenical cooperation. The international character of sports facilitates inter-religious contact and dialogue, and often provides a first contact with the Muslim or Buddhist religion, not to forget the many Jewish communities and organisations.

The world of sports also brings to light many new problems and challenges to be faced by society as a whole. In this way, sport functions as a seismograph for social developments and challenges. This means that the Church can use the world of sport to detect problems and act accordingly. In order to strengthen and to continue the Church's pastoral guidance and missionary presence in the world of sports, it would be advisable to establish institutional contact with the international sports federations. Moreover, those working as sport chaplains are advised to find ways to enter into a dialogue with this institutions, not only at the national, but also at the international level. Such an exchange of ideas and experiences would help to intensify the Church's commitment to sports. This is presently practised in the pastoral commission of FICEP (an International Federation of Catholic Sports Organisations, of which DJK is a member). Cooperation with the national bishops' conferences is indispensable, especially because they also need to establish contact with the national sports federations.

With regard to the FIFA World Cup in Germany next year, I wish to illustrate with the help of some selected examples that major sporting events can also have an emanating effect through to the local communities and therefore can be taken up by the parishes to fulfil their social tasks. Both the Catholic Church in Germany and the Evangelical Church take up the watchwords of the World Cup: "A time to make friends" and are doing everything possible to help make it an event marked by hospitality. Our parishes will offer liturgical services (if possible, in the native languages of the respective guests), they will offer pastoral guidance for the teams from abroad, and they will welcome visitors by means of the coordinated "Open Churches" project. There are various possibilities for parishes to invite people to meet, talk, get to know each other and to accommodate guests. The broad field of youth ministry (which was already tried and tested during World Youth Day!) will be involved as well as the major relief agencies of the Church (Adveniat, Misereor, etc.) which give great importance to sport in their international activities.

These are only a few examples for the Church's commitment to fostering a presence at major sporting events. But, based on experience, we can say that Catholic sport chaplains provide a great opportunity for the Church to realize her mission in the modern world.

The challenges of being a Christian athlete

As I love playing sports I always knew they would be a part of my life. When I was eight years old – just like all other boys at this age – I wanted to be a major league baseball player. I did not want this because of money or fame; rather, I wanted to be a ballplayer because I felt that this was what God wanted me to do. I felt it was a calling! Having attended *Crespi Catholic High School,* an all-boys Carmelite school in California with an active retreat program, I was able to grow in my knowledge of the faith. During my senior year while on one of those retreats, I had a very spiritual experience before a large wooden cross. In that moment of prayer, I asked God to give me the strength to be able to accept his will for my life. I thought He was leading me towards baseball, but I wasn't sure. So I put it all into his hands and here I am today! I would like to share with you some of the challenges and opportunities that I face as a Catholic player in professional sports.

I have often been asked: "What are the challenges you face as a professional athlete?" I usually respond: "The same challenges as everybody else!" People tend to put professional athletes on a different level, yet, we have to face the same challenges in life as everyone else. After graduating from high school, I left a distinctly Catholic environment and entered a world where I continually came into contact with people of different faiths, many of whom challenged my own

---

* Since 1993, Jeff Suppan has been a pitcher in Major League Baseball: first with the Boston Red Sox, and since 2004, for the St. Louis Cardinals. He has had successive winning seasons with the Cardinals and ended the 2005 season with an E.R.A. (earned run average) of 3.57, among the best in his league, which also brought the Cardinals to the playoffs for the World Series.

faith. As a young ballplayer, I was trying to focus on my talent, leaving me little time to study the faith. Yet, in the clubhouse, many different opinions on faith and beliefs came into discussion. One time, after getting into a lively debate with a fellow player, I had to finally tell him that we should table our discussion in order to be able to work together as a team.

Another challenge is that of constant travel as I no longer had my local parish. When I had questions about the faith or needed guidance, I could no longer go to the priest I had known all my life. I was constantly meeting new priests and parishes but always just "passing through". The real challenge was just getting to Mass on Sunday! A Major League schedule consists or 162 games in 6 months, plus a month of Spring Training in Florida. We play from coast to coast moving from city to city on nearly a daily basis: a lot of games, travelling, time zones and hotels! Waking up early after a late night game is difficult and not good before a game. It is definitely a challenge for professional Catholic athletes to attend Sunday Mass during the season. Finding a priest in order to go to Confession can be a challenge as well. In some Catholic cities, like Boston, it is much easier than others. There have been times when I just had to call up any parish I could find in the phone book to arrange for confession.

One opportunity available to a professional athlete is media exposure which is definitively a means to reach a lot of people. It is such a responsibility and I want to be the best role model I can in order to lead them to follow Jesus. It's amazing how children listen to us! On one occasion, I was telling some elementary students a story about following Jesus and what they should try to do to be good and to live good lives. It was during the time of the conclave and the next day the teacher told them about how the Cardinals pick a new pope from among the Cardinals. One of the little first graders raised her hand and said: "I think they should pick Jeff Suppan – he is a great Cardinal!"

Yet, media exposure is a very brief opportunity as a professional athlete normally has such a short career: three years is the average career of a major league baseball player and ten years is exceptional. It is such a short window of opportunity to reach the people you can while you are an active player. Of course there is life after baseball. But, the time you have as a current player, when children and fans are watching you and when your influence is at its peak, ends all-too-soon.

Although full of challenges, my professional career has also given me opportunities to grow in my faith. Listening to other people who questioned my faith, I did not always know how to respond to these questions; I just believed. Yet this is not always the most compelling response to a sceptic! So, I started to learn about apologetics. In speaking to students, especially in Catholic high schools, I will throw in some apologetics. Because professional athletes are able to attract the attention of their audience, we can help others in their faith. Apologetics is also a way to reach out to Catholic professional athletes in order to help them know and defend their faith. My mother (who attended Catholic school before the second Vatican Council) said that she had studied apologetics in school. Yet, I had never heard of the word before, nor knew what a powerful tool it could be until I was directly questioned about my faith and had to find the answers on my own.

Another key that helped me to grow in my faith was discovering the value of a spiritual advisor. Ten years ago, when I was in Boston, I met an *Opus Dei* priest, Fr. Dick Reiman. He became my spiritual advisor which was a new and great experience. In fact, we still talk to this day and it is a great asset. Through spiritual direction I came to understand better the importance of confession and the need to examine my conscience so that I would be able to live, or try to live, like Christ. I know that not every player can have an individual priest to attend to them, but perhaps there could be a priest available for an entire team. Having a priest as a chaplain to a team of professional athletes could provide them with this opportunity.

Sharing my faith with others has been another way of growing in it. I tried to explain my faith in the Church in a nice way. I went to many Bible studies in my baseball career. Yet, unfortunately it seemed that everybody was against me. Often I would say in exasperation: "I thought we were here to talk about Jesus!" As I did not want to be converted to another faith, I stopped going to bible studies and just went to Mass more often, which was great. The daily reading of Scripture has really helped my spiritual life. I came across the monthly publication of the *The Magnificat* –a daily reading and meditation on the liturgy of the day- which has been really beneficial for me. It is a pity, however, that as Christians we can't simply gather to focus on the gospel and on Jesus in a peaceful setting.

As Catholic athletes we tend to be very private in our faith. We also need help to learn how to evangelize as we often don't know how to do it. We need help to know how to use our place in the modern culture for His benefit and that of the Church. Yet, I believe that we will step up to the plate and face these challenges if we are guided. There are many Catholics who are very strong in their faith but do not have a way to reach people. Furthermore, the media sometimes portrays some of us in different way than we really are. They can tend to focus on the negative as society feeds on that. However, the majority of players, with their good deeds, go unrecognized while the minority get the attention. Much of this is beyond our control. However, I am confident that we can come up with some initiatives that can help athletes spread the message of Jesus Christ. I believe that we can do it by working together. By learning the most effective ways to do so we can really make a difference.

TABLE OF CONTENTS

I. Round Table
Problems and challenges in sports today

II. Round Table
Sport: frontier of the new evangelisation

PUBLICATIONS
OF THE PONTIFICAL COUNCIL FOR THE LAITY

Publications by the Pontifical Council for the Laity are generally issued in Italian, English, French and Spanish and occasionally in other languages. Their contents emerge from events held by the dicastery (conferences, seminars, plenary assemblies...) that deal with the apostolate of the laity, and also Youth Section activities including the International Youth Forum and World Youth Day. They can be obtained from the Pontifical Council for the Laity offices.

Notiziario - News

Biannual newsletter with information on activities of the Pontifical Council for the Laity. Published in English, French, Italian and Spanish (annual subscription including postage: € 5,00)

"Laity Today" collection

1. *Rediscovering Baptism*, 17th Plenary Assembly, 27-31 October 1997 (€ 10,00)

2. *Movements in the Church,* world congress of ecclesial movements, 27-29 May 1998 (€ 10,00) Available in English and Italian only.

3. *Rediscovering Confirmation,* 18th Plenary Assembly, 27 February - 2 March 1999 (€ 10,00)

4. *The Ecclesial Movements in the Pastoral Concern of the Bishops,* Seminar, 16-18 June 1999 (€ 10,00)

5. *The Congress of Catholic Laity - Rome 2000,* International Congress, 25-30 November 2000 (€ 10,00)

6. *Ecumenismo e dialogo interreligioso: il contributo dei fedeli laici.* Seminar, 22-23 June 2001 (€ 10,00). Available in Italian only.

7. *Rediscovering the Eucharist,* 20th Plenary Assembly, 21-23 November 2002 (€ 6,00)

8. *Men and women: reciprocal complementarity,* Seminar, 30-31 January 2004 (€ 10,00) Available in English and Italian only.

9. *Riscoprire il vero volto della parocchia (Rediscovering the true face of the parish),* 21st Plenary Assembly, 25-27 November 2004 (€ 10,00). Available in Italian only.

"Youth" collection

1. *Together on the European Roads,* 3rd European Meeting on Youth Ministry, 21-24 September 1998 (€ 10,00)

2. *Youth Jubilee - Rome 2000,* 7th International Youth Forum and 15th World Youth Day, 12-20 August 2000 (€ 10,00)

3. *Youth and University: witnessing to Christ in the university world,* 8th International Youth Forum, 31 March - 4 April 2004 (€ 10,00)

Documents

– *Directory of international associations of the lay faithful* (2004) (€ 10,00)

– *The Dignity of Older People and their Mission in the Church and in the World,* 1998 (€ 5,00)

– *The Pontifical Council for the Laity* (1997) (€ 5,00)

Photographic albums

– *The Pope and the Movements. Together,* Rome, 30 May 1998 (€ 5,00)

– *Youth and University: witnessing to Christ in the university world, International Youth Forum, Rocca di Papa (Rome), 31 March – 4 April 2004* (€ 5,00)

Other publications

I Care, the magazine of the Youth Section of the Pontifical Council for the Laity published in English, French, Italian and Spanish by the *Youth Church Hope* Foundation before and after each WYD:

– n. 14, April 2005 (€ 5,00)

– n. 15, December 2005 (€ 5,00)

Earlier publications are still available from our offices. These are publications by the Youth Section related to events prior to 1997: Proceedings of Meetings, international youth forums and World Youth Day.

– *"I am the Way, the Truth and the Life"*, Santiago de Compostela, 13-15 August 1989.

– *What do you seek, young pilgrims?*, Santiago de Compostela, 15-20 August 1989.

– *The spirit of the sons and daughters of God: spirit of freedom*, Czestochowa, 7-10 August 1991.

– *"You have received a spirit of sonship"*, Czestochowa, 10-15 August 1991.

– *"I came that they might have life"*, Denver, 7-15 August 1993.

– *Together on the European roads*, 1st European meeting on youth ministry, Rome 23-27 May 1994.

– *"As the Father sent me so I am sending you"*, Manila, 6-15 January 1995.

– *Together on the European roads*, 2nd European meeting on youth ministry, Loreto, 12-16 September 1995.

– *"Teacher, where are you staying? Come and see"*, Paris, 14-24 August 1997.

* * *

Postal address: Pontificio Consiglio per i Laici
Palazzo San Calisto
00120 CITTÀ DEL VATICANO

Officies: Piazza San Calisto, 16 (Trastevere)
00153 ROMA

Tel.: 06 69887322
Fax: 06 69887214
E-mail: pcpl@laity.va
Telegrammi: Consilaic

VATICAN PRESS